Mark Twain's Civil War

Mark Twain's Civil War

"The Private History of a Campaign That Failed"

Edited by Benjamin Griffin
of the Mark Twain Project

With maps by Mark Twain
and illustrations by E. W. Kemble

Heyday, Berkeley, California

The Bancroft Library, University of California,
Berkeley, California

Library of Congress Cataloging-in-Publication Data
Names: Twain, Mark, 1835-1910, author. | Griffin, Benjamin, 1968-, editor. |
    Kemble, E. W. (Edward Windsor), 1861-1933, illustrator.
Title: Mark Twain's Civil War : "The private history of a campaign that
    failed" / edited by Benjamin Griffin, of the Mark Twain Project, with maps
    by Mark Twain and illustrations by E. W. Kemble.
Other titles: Private history of a campaign that failed
Description: Berkeley, CA : Heyday, 2019. | Includes bibliographical
    references.
Identifiers: LCCN 2019021570 | ISBN 9781597144780 (hardcover : alk. paper)
Subjects: LCSH: United States--History--Civil War, 1861-1865--Fiction. |
    Soldiers--Confederate States of America--Fiction. | United
    States--History--Civil War, 1861-1865--Literature and the war. | GSAFD:
    Autobiographical fiction. | Historical fiction | War stories.
Classification: LCC PS1322 .P75 2019 | DDC 813/.4--dc23
LC record available at https://lccn.loc.gov/2019021570

Book design: Ashley Ingram
Cover image: Samuel L. Clemens, 1851 or 1852. From a photographic print in the
    Mark Twain Papers.
Endpapers: detail of *Bird's Eye View of Saint Louis, Mo.*, lithograph by J. T. Palmatary,
    1858.
Frontispiece: Samuel L. Clemens, 1858. Vassar College Library.

Published by Heyday
P.O. Box 9145, Berkeley, California 94709
(510) 549-3564
www.heydaybooks.com

Printed in Stevens Point, Wisconsin, by Worzalla

10 9 8 7 6 5 4 3 2 1

CONTENTS

ACKNOWLEDGMENTS

Although this volume was not proposed to the National Endowment for the Humanities or specifically funded by it, I wish to begin by acknowledging the agency's long-standing support—meaning also the American taxpayers' support—for the Mark Twain Papers and Project. Generous assistance has also come from individual donors too numerous to list here; from the members of the Mark Twain Luncheon Club and its directors, Roger Samuelsen, Robert Middlekauff, and Watson M. (Mac) Laetsch; from the University of California, Berkeley, Class of 1958; and from the Friends of The Bancroft Library. Thanks also to the staff of the Library of the University of California; to the University Librarian, Jeffrey MacKie-Mason; to Elaine C. Tennant, the James D. Hart Director of The Bancroft Library, who has spared no effort in helping this book into print; and to Peter E. Hanff, Deputy Director of The Bancroft Library, and a trusted advisor.

My colleagues at the Mark Twain Project rendered substantial help. Harriet Elinor Smith brought her expected, but always appreciated, rigor to a thorough reformation of the introduction and notes, and helped me verify the accuracy of the text. Mandy Gagel fact-checked the introduction and notes. Melissa Martin, in addition to her contributions as the Project's administrative officer, has here an editorial role as transcriber of a challenging newspaper facsimile. They have my admiring gratitude.

Without the assistance of several institutions, much that is here would have been lacking. I mean the State Historical Society of Missouri (both in Columbia and in St. Louis); the Library and Research Center of the Missouri Historical Society, St. Louis; and the University of Maryland Library, College Park. For images and permission to reprint I am happily indebted to the Mark Twain Boyhood Home and Museum, Hannibal, Missouri; the Washington University Libraries, St. Louis; Vassar College Library, Poughkeepsie, New York; the American Civil War Museum, Richmond, Virginia; and the Library of Congress in Washington, D.C. For permission to reprint copyrighted writings, thanks are due, as ever, to the Mark Twain Foundation. And it is a pleasure to acknowledge the publishing house Heyday, of Berkeley; its far-seeing publisher, Steve Wasserman; and editor Lisa K. Marietta, who has furnished thorough and valuable copy-editing.

Finally, Kathleen Ryan heard patiently the accumulating particulars of research into the gun battery at Vicksburg, the life of Absalom Grimes, and the gravel road between Hannibal and New London, as if such things could have been in any way expected.

B.G.

INTRODUCTION

In 1877 a New York journalist was shocked to learn the fact, not widely known at the time, that Mark Twain had been a rebel soldier in the Civil War. "Surely an explanation is in order," he wrote; "perhaps it was all a joke."[1] Eight years would pass before Mark Twain published his explanation, a magazine article entitled "The Private History of a Campaign That Failed." Ostensibly this told what he did in the war, or, in his own words, why he "didn't do anything" in it; but the article was criticized as disingenuous and disrespectful, and it did little to address a growing curiosity about the nature of his brief and inconsequential military service. Keen to enlist but sedulously avoiding combat, his abandonment of the rebellion has been denounced as cowardice—also praised as enlightened self-interest, and even as pacifism. The complex political situation in Missouri during the early months of the war, and Mark Twain's genius for transforming life into fiction, have tended to obstruct historical understanding of "The Private History"; but a fresh look at the well-known story, informed by newly recovered sources, now sheds light on Mark Twain's Civil War, and on its emergence as a topic in his life and writing.

Born and raised in the slaveholding state of Missouri, Mark Twain (Samuel Langhorne Clemens, 1835–1910) absorbed the political and racial attitudes typical of his class and region. A single anecdote can help to clarify the Southernness of this

1. Untitled item, New York *World*, 25 Jan 1877, 4.

Hannibal, Missouri, household—as when we read that Clemens's parents, emigrants from the states of Virginia and Kentucky, used to manage their slave Jenny "by threats to 'Rent her to the Yankees.'"[2] The farm of his aunt and uncle in Monroe County, where he spent his summers, was worked by slaves.[3] In maturity, Clemens believed that he had been trained by society to approve slavery, and that "training" (a favorite word) "is all there is *to* a person."[4] The appeal to training offers to extenuate his complicity in slavery, but it is powerless to explain how Clemens came to "modify" (another favorite word) the attitudes to which he was trained. Over time, he would repudiate slaveholding society and set down some of literature's most searing critiques of slavery and race prejudice. There is abundant evidence for the change in his views, although the attempt to plot its development as a straightforward progress comes to grief on account of his strangely self-contradictory mental organization. Accepted in his own time as a model "reconstructed rebel," how he measures up to evolving standards is a larger subject, with a history of its own.[5]

2. Webster 1918, 14, quoted in *Inds*, 327. On slavery in Hannibal, see Dempsey 2003. The first chapter of Michael Fellman's *Inside War* summarizes the social and political makeup of pre–Civil War Missouri (Fellman 1989, 1–22).

3. *AutoMT1*, 210–12; Dempsey 2003, 15–16.

4. *A Connecticut Yankee in King Arthur's Court* (1889), chap. 18.

5. Studies of Mark Twain in relation to African Americans, slavery, and the South include Pettit 1974, Fishkin 1993 and 1997, Chadwick-Joshua 1998, and Dempsey 2003. Studies of Mark Twain and the Civil War include Lorch 1941, Cox 1966 (chap. 8), Mattson 1968a, Schmitz

1. "The boys are responding bravely"

From September 1860 to May 1861 Clemens was a pilot on the steamboat *Alonzo Child*, plying the Mississippi River between New Orleans and St. Louis. He had two co-pilots: Horace E. Bixby, from western New York, who had "learned him the river" between 1857 and 1859, and Will Bowen, a Hannibal contemporary.[6] In "The Private History," Clemens tells us that at the time of South Carolina's secession, he was "strong for the Union," and his Unionism is glimpsed in a letter by his mother, which relates that "when Sam and W[ill] B[owen] were on the Alonzo Chi they quarreled and Sam let go the wheel to whip Will for talking secesh and made Will hush."[7] It is important to note that Unionism did not necessarily entail either opposition to slavery or friendliness to the Northern states. Clemens could, for example, have been a "conditional Unionist," opposed to secession, but only as long as the government refrained from "coercion" of the slave states. In the presidential election of 1860 Clemens supported John Bell and Edward Everett, the candidates of the newly founded Constitutional Unionist party. The platform of this ostensibly non-partisan party recognized "no political principle other than the Constitution of the country, the Union of the States, and the enforcement of the laws." This

---

1995, Messent 2001 (chap. 8), Rachels 2007, Fulton 2010, Loving 2013, and Scharnhorst 2018 (chap. 6).

6. For Horace E. Bixby and Will Bowen, see pp. 113–14, note on 80.1.

7. Jane Lampton Clemens to "all in the Territory," 12 and 14 Oct 1862, NPV, quoted in *L1,* 213 n. 22.

Steamboats at the St. Louis riverfront, including the *Alonzo Child*.
Detail of a lithograph by J. T. Palmatary, 1858.

was a refusal to grant that the status of slavery in the United
States and its territories had become a constitutional crisis. Bell's
speeches implied that the Constitution could be counted on
to protect and expand Southern slavery; and Bell–Everett was
the ticket favored in the most intensively slaveholding areas of
Missouri, where plantation owners hoped to preserve the Union,
with slavery, and without a war.[8]

When the *Alonzo Child* left St. Louis for New Orleans on
14 January 1861, the state of Mississippi had just seceded. At

8.   *MTBus*, 47; Snead 1886, 54–57; Fellman 1989, 5; Dempsey 2003,
256–61; "What Bell and Everett Say," Glasgow (Mo.) *Weekly Times*, 23
Aug 1860, 3.

Vicksburg a battery of guns was compelling boats to come to shore and be searched. The state's governor hoped to intercept a shipment of artillery believed to have been sent to Southern military forts by the recently resigned secretary of war, John B. Floyd. The *Alonzo Child* passed this blockade at one o'clock in the morning on 22 January, an event recalled by Will Bowen in an 1889 letter to Clemens:

> Do you recall the first Gun of the war directed *at you* from Vicksburg Fort, expecting to capture the Boat that had Floyds Pittsburg armament, going to Baton Rouge. You were on watch on the "Alonzo Child^s."[9]

Clemens was in New Orleans on 26 January, when Louisiana went out of the Union. He recalled the occasion in notebook entries made almost half a century later: "Great rejoicing. Flags, Dixie, soldiers."[10] In "The Private History" he tells us he was now "a rebel," connecting his conversion with the fact

9. Bowen to SLC, 10 Dec 1889, CU-MARK. The Vicksburg gun battery was in place from 12 January until at least 24 January (Marleau 2015, 71–75; "Steamboat Calendar: Clemens's Piloting Assignments, 1857–1861," *L1*, 389; Scharf 1887, 240; "From Mississippi," Nashville *Patriot*, 12 Jan 1861, extra; "The Big Guns at Vicksburg," Louisville *Courier*, 22 Jan 1861, 4; "River Intelligence," New Orleans *Crescent*, 23 Jan 1861, 1; "The Blockade of the Mississippi," Cleveland *Leader*, 23 Jan 1861, 3; "The Mississippi River Blockade," Philadelphia *Inquirer*, 24 Jan 1861, 1, reprinting the Memphis *Appeal* of 17 Jan; "The Mississippi Blockade," New York *Evening Post*, 26 Jan 1861, 3).

10. Notebook 48, TS p. 8 (CU-MARK). A reference in a nearby entry dates this cluster of Civil War reminiscences to around November 1908.

that at this time "the secession atmosphere had considerably thickened on the Lower Mississippi"; he might have added that it was especially thick in the steamboating business.[11] The next day, Clemens paid a social visit to the home of a prominent steamboatman of New Orleans. John A. Stevenson was secretary of the Pilots' Benevolent Association, the trade union of pilots in the St. Louis–New Orleans trade.[12] In a recently discovered letter

11. It was the testimony of one pilot that "the whole of the Saint Louis and New Orleans pilots, one hundred and twenty-eight, (128,) except five (5,) were disunion," and that, as the war approached, his fellow pilots threatened him that if he sided with the North he "would never be allowed to pilot any more, let it end as it would." This threat was carried out after the war: "A steamboat-agent in New Orleans told me he would not ship freight on a boat that I was connected with, and would use his best influence to prevent others also. His name is John A. Stevenson, of New Orleans" (U.S. House of Representatives 1876, 117; see also U.S. House of Representatives 1866, 53–54).

12. Stevenson (1822–1901) was a pilot and captain on the Mississippi from 1850, and became secretary of the Pilots' Association on its formation in 1857. It is not clear whether Clemens met up with Stevenson during his 1882 visit to New Orleans; he later obtained from Stevenson a copy of his own "first" newspaper article for use in *Life on the Mississippi*. Mark Twain gave a sketch of the Pilots' Association in "Old Times on the Mississippi" (SLC 1875e, revised as SLC 1883, chap. 15; *N&J1*, 58–59; Kruse 1981, 84–89; Memphis *Appeal*: "River Matters," 5 Sept 1857, 5; "General News," 5 May 1882, 3; "River News," New Orleans *Democrat*, 11 Apr 1880, 7; 19 July 1882 to Osgood, CtY-BR, in *MTLP*, 156–57; New Orleans *Picayune*: "The River," 8 May 1882, 2; "Captain John A. Stevenson," 5 Apr 1901, 7). Several sources (including *N&J1*, 58 n. 8) confuse Stevenson of the Pilots' Association with another Captain John A. Stevenson (1818–84), who was a cotton merchant, designer of the rebel ram *Manassas*, and a Republican candidate for governor of Louisiana in 1884; or with that man's son, also named John A. Stevenson (1842–96; "Death of John A. Stevenson," New Orleans *Picayune*, 4 Nov 1896, 3).

dated 27 January, Clemens sketches the Stevenson household, conveying a strong sense of excitement in the wake of secession. As this letter has never been published, a transcription is given here of as much of the text as has been recovered. Clemens writes from the St. Louis Hotel. Located in the French Quarter, near the headquarters of the Pilots' Association, it was popular with New Orleans's planter and business aristocracy, and a premier venue for slave auctions.[13]

> St. Louis Hotel,
> New Orleans, Jan. 27,

> Latest from the Seat of War!
> Express from St. Mary street!
> No Lives Lost! &c. &c.

Dear Beaman:

We—Thrall and I,—have just arrived, per horse railroad—(free passage, too—though why they should compliment *us* in this way surpasses my com (d—n such a pen,) prehension,)—horse railroad, I believe I said—(and most infernal cars they *do* have on their street railroads here; with three compartments in them, respectively for gentlemen, ladies, and servants; and a bench running fore-and-aft on the hurricane deck for *other* people—and we occupied that bench,) and—per horse railroad, you know, from St. Mary street, N$^{o.}$ 350,—on the gate—(but you don't find the house by the *number*, Beaman—ah, no—look for the benches over the gutter—Stephenson's house is abreast the bench which

13. Campanella 2015.

isn't painted—and mind, if it's in the night, Stanard, Beware of the Dog.—not a poodle dog, nor a spaniel, nor a "Terrier;" nor any other species of the docile, undecided sort of dog—but a most astonishingly developed, and wonderfully matter-of-fact brute of the Newfoundland persuasion, who don't care a * * for anybody's arguments after dark—and this reminds me of those beautiful lines of Gray's—(you'll find them in his "Elegy in a—well, really, now, I am not right sure—though it runs in my head that it *was*,—in a Brick-yard.")—never mind that, though—*n'importe*—read the poetry:

> "Homeward the plowman plods his weary way,
> And wastes his sweetness on the desert air."

Capital, ain't they? But they don't sound—that is to say, ex—but no matter how they sound, you know—*Dogs* is the question—and while I am on the subject I may as well mention that "Secession"—that's the oldest pup—(and the pride of the family—so I was informed by Miss Lizzie Stephenson,) is—*dead*—melancholy, but true. Blast the dog, he *would* eat indigestible food, and so the "dangrey"* got him. The other two pups, named respectively "Venus" and ["]Pilot," and aged about the same as their deceased brother, are doing well—remarkably well—as Miss P-i-d-g-e— pidge—(right, I believe)—told me—and she told me also to— Now what in the world *did* that lovely damsel tell me—unclear— it might have been something concerning a *bet* that Stanard made about Miss Pidgeon's marriage, and "which" that delightful young bird imagines he is sorry he ever made it, (and she isn't married yet—but she ought to be, for she is a good girl,—and pretty.) But not nearly so pretty as *Babe*, though.—(indeed—and I only

---

* "Break-bone fever." [*Clemens's footnote*]

whisper it—in the subscriber's opinion—*that* Infant is a Stunner)
Yes, she is—Stunner's the *word*. She is *very* pretty—but I'll *swear* I
used to think the other the handsomest— d—n the italics—they
slip in without my knowledge sometimes.

Glancing back over my letter, there seems to be too much information, and not enough comment—which is bad—and reminds
me of the ship captain who gave his steward fifteen dollars to buy
provisions with, for a long voyage—and told

[one page of text is unrecovered]

P. S.

Beaman, you'll do to read the Newcomes. Why when I read
your letter to Thrall, and lingered over that portion of it which
portrayed so lucidly the relationship existing between Joel and
Reuben, and Louisa B., &c., &c., and not a single blunder in it, I
envied you your talent for dissecting kinsmanship—while a troop
of uneasy phantoms from the Newcomes straggled through my
brain, and I saw poor Ethel, who was Clive's grandmother, you
know—and Lady Kew, who was sister to Lord Farintosh—and
Rosa, who was kin to somebody—and Old Tom, and the Colonel and Lady Clara, and the brave old hero of a hundred Indian
battles, Barnes Newcome, Jr., and the old gentleman who said
"Adsum," when his name was called, &c., &c., &c.,—mixed—
mixed—mixed—in dire confusion—so to remain forever and
ever. *How* can a man ever understand that book?

Sam. Clemens[14]

14. This letter, which came to light in 2015, is in a private collection.
Clemens begins it with a volley of journalistic clichés: "Latest from the Seat
of War!" is topical, as war was generally anticipated in January 1861, while
"No Lives Lost!" is typical of steamboat accident reports. Few of the people

Six states had now seceded, and Missouri's governor, Claiborne Fox Jackson (1806–62), meant for Missouri to join them. The state legislature was mostly with him: in January it had passed a resolution stating that if any slave states should be invaded, "the people of Missouri will instantly rally on the side of their Southern brethren to resist the invaders," and it called a state legislative convention to consider the question of secession. But when the people of Missouri chose delegates to this convention, not a single avowed secessionist was among their number; the prospect of legal secession was doomed before the convention began. Governor Jackson's friends now placed their hopes in the so-called Military Bill, written by Marion County state representative Thomas A. Harris, which proposed to reform the existing militia as an army commanded by the governor and loyal to him alone.[15]

On 12 April 1861, the federal garrison at Fort Sumter, under siege since December 1860, was fired on by Confederate forces.

---

mentioned in the letter have been identified. John A. Stevenson lived at 350 St. Mary Street with his wife, Lizzie; two daughters, Lizzie W. (born ca. 1858) and Annie (born ca. 1860); and three of his wife's female relatives (Gardner 1861, 418; *Orleans Census* 1860, 758). Clemens mentions: New Orleans's system of horse-car railroads, still under construction at the time; Thomas Gray's "Elegy Written in a Country Churchyard" (1751); "the dangrey," i.e., dengue fever, a mosquito-borne illness; and Thackeray's novel *The Newcomes* (1854–55) ("Horse Railroads in New Orleans," New Orleans *Picayune*, 21 Apr 1861, 1).

15. Snead 1886, 46–47, 50–52, 66–77, 106. For Harris's biography, see pp. 123–25, note on 101.13.

President Lincoln called on state governors to send troops to put down the rebellion; Missouri's share would be 3,123 troops. Jackson replied: "Your requisition is illegal, unconstitutional and revolutionary; in its object inhuman & diabolical. Not one man will Missouri furnish to carry on any such unholy crusade against her Southern sisters."[16] Nearly fifty years later, Clemens remembered that he had heard of the firing on Fort Sumter while aboard the *Alonzo Child*, "at Vicksburg on way down (the day after it happened)," and he remembered the crew's reaction: "We hoisted stars & bars & played Dixie."[17] The boat steamed into New Orleans on 16 April, one river journalist hailing the rebel flag streaming from her jackstaff as a "sign of the times" and assuring his readers that she was owned and operated by "true-hearted Southrons."[18] The *Child* departed New Orleans

16. Phillips 2000, 245.

17. In his notebook Clemens writes that the news reached him on "April 18." This is an error for "April 13," which was "the day after it happened," the day the news reached Vicksburg, and a plausible day for the *Alonzo Child* to pass that city "on way down" (Notebook 48, TS p. 9, CU-MARK; "Steamboat Calendar: Clemens's Piloting Assignments, 1857–1861," *L1*, 390; "The War News," Vicksburg [Miss.] *Evening Citizen*, 13 Apr 1861, 2; "Steamboats," New Orleans *Picayune*, 18 Apr 1861, 4). The *Alonzo Child*'s twenty-eight-foot Confederate flag had been presented in March by a party of "loyal southern ladies" to the boat's captain, David DeHaven, an "intense secessionist" who "wanted the South to get her rights, and to be let alone" ("River News," St. Louis *Missouri Republican*, 20 Mar 1861, 4; "Letter from the *Alonzo Child*," St. Louis *Missouri State Journal*, 8 Apr 1861, 1; "River News and Steamboat Business," Memphis *Appeal*, 27 Nov 1861, 4, reprinting the St. Louis *Democrat* of 19 Nov).

18. "River Intelligence," New Orleans *Crescent*, 17 Apr 1861, 8; Marleau 2015, 76–78. In January 1862 another Confederate flag would

again on 18 April. Clemens planned, on arrival in St. Louis, to make a side excursion to Hannibal, collect a debt, and return to St. Louis in time for the boat's trip to New Orleans. He dashed off a letter to his brother, Orion, to this effect, ending with an urgent request: "Orion bring down 'Armageddon' with you if you have it. If not, *buy* it." Someone must have recommended this eccentric book, which marshalled biblical evidence to prove that the final battle between good and evil would soon take place in the Mississippi River Valley.[19]

The presumption that Clemens was aboard the *Alonzo Child* when she left St. Louis for New Orleans on 2 May has bred speculation on how he later got back to Missouri amid the disturbances of the war.[20] As a matter of fact, we do not know

be presented to Captain DeHaven, this one by none other than fugitive governor Claiborne Jackson ("Affairs at New Orleans," New York *Herald*, 18 Jan 1862, 8).

19. 26 Apr 1861 to OC, *L1*, 120–21 n. 3. *Armageddon* (1854) was written by the Southern Methodist minister Samuel D. Baldwin (1818–66). Baldwin was also the author of *Dominion* (1857), a defense of slavery arguing from biblical principles ("Death of Dr. Baldwin," Augusta [Ga.] *Constitutionalist*, 14 Oct 1866, 3).

20. It is often stated as fact that Clemens returned to Missouri on the steamboat *Nebraska*, which left New Orleans on 14 May and arrived in St. Louis on 21 May. This is conjecture, based, at several removes, on the official biography of Mark Twain by Albert Bigelow Paine (1861–1937). Paine wrote that Clemens went up as a passenger on the *Uncle Sam*; that it was piloted by Zeb Leavenworth; that it was fired on at Jefferson Barracks, twelve miles below St. Louis; and that it was "the last steamboat to make the trip from New Orleans to St. Louis" (*MTB*, 1:161–62). This narrative, discounted by Fred Lorch in 1941, received a selective rehabilitation from J. Stanley Mattson in 1968. Retaining only the "last boat through" detail,

with any assurance that he made the trip down at all. Will Bowen had left and gone home in April, and Clemens may well have

Mattson reasoned that Clemens went up on the *Nebraska*, said to have been the last boat to evade what Mattson called "the Union blockade at Memphis." (That blockade was, of course, Confederate.) He ignores the fact that no report of the *Nebraska*'s arrival mentions artillery fire or damage, and he ignores the anomalous presence of Zeb Leavenworth, not otherwise found piloting the *Nebraska*; he is found back in March 1861 on his usual craft, the *John J. Roe*. Unfortunately, Edgar Marquess Branch relied on Mattson in his chronicle of Clemens's piloting career, as well as in his contribution to *Mark Twain's Letters, Volume 1* (Lorch 1941, 460–61; Mattson 1968b, 405, 406–7; Branch 1986; *L1*: 121, and "Steamboat Calendar: Clemens's Piloting Assignments, 1857–1861," 385–90; Marleau 2015, 81–84; "River Intelligence," New Orleans *Crescent*, 21 Mar 1861, 8; "A Southern Blockade at Memphis," Philadelphia *Inquirer*, 22 May 1861, 1; "Affairs at Camp Defiance," New York *Herald*, 26 May 1861, 4; "From Cairo," New York *Times*, 29 May 1861, 9; "Affairs up the River," New Orleans *Picayune*, 30 Apr 1861, 2).

Paine's informant was surely Clemens, whose own accounts of his exit from the river are similarly incoherent. His 1899 autobiographical notes say he "started North" on 27 January 1861, his boat being damaged by artillery fire at Jefferson Barracks (*AutoMT3*, 652; cf. Notebook 48, TS p. 8 [CU-MARK]); actually, Clemens and the *Alonzo Child* continued regular service, undamaged, for months after January. In a 1901 letter he said that "when Louisiana went out of the Union on the 26th day of January, 1861, the crew [of the *Alonzo Child*] were paid off and she entered the Confederate service....I returned home on the 'A. T. Lacey' and escaped the blockade at Memphis, by only a couple of hours" (21 Jan 1901 to Sarah H. Godfrey, ViU). In fact, the Memphis blockade and the seizure of the *Alonzo Child* by the Confederacy happened months after Louisiana's secession, and the *A. T. Lacey* had been destroyed in 1860 ("Camp Defiance Intelligence," New York *Herald*, 2 June 1861, 8; "Disasters in 1860," New Orleans *True Delta*, 10 Jan 1861, 3; "The Seizure of Boats," Richmond [Va.] *Enquirer*, 31 May 1861, 4; "The War News," Davenport [Iowa] *Quad-City Times*, 24 May 1861, 2).

followed suit.[21] The state of the river was unsettled, and traffic was slowing to a trickle. A St. Louis journalist wrote that "the war news has completely upset the course of trade; no one seems disposed to operate, and our boating interest is entirely cut up and done for."[22] Once back in New Orleans, the *Alonzo Child*'s owners decided to run her in the New Orleans–Memphis trade, to save her from seizure by the Union; on her first trip up, she was seized by the Confederacy.[23]

21. 26 Apr 1861 to OC, *L1*, 120–21 n. 2.

22. "River Intelligence," New Orleans *Delta*, 1 May 1861, 4.

23. The *Alonzo Child* was impounded at Memphis by the Confederate general Gideon Pillow around 23 May 1861. Captain DeHaven reached an accommodation with the Confederates, and the *Child* carried both troops and commercial passengers between Memphis and New Orleans until 1862, when he sold her to the rebel navy. He next built gunboats at the Confederate navy yard in Selma, Alabama. In 1876 DeHaven, brazenly posing as a lifelong Unionist, petitioned the United States government, seeking $50,000 compensation for his loss of the *Alonzo Child* to the Confederates. The claim was disallowed when the War Department supplied evidence of the petitioner's disloyalty and his previous compensation by the Confederacy. By that time DeHaven had died of typhoid fever (U.S. Senate 1876; U.S. Senate 1877; Bofinger 1877; Hardy 1879, 47–48; DeHaven 1913, 194; "River Intelligence," New Orleans *Crescent*, 23 May 1861, 1; "The War News," Davenport [Iowa] *Quad-City Times*, 24 May 1861, 2; "The steamer Alonzo Child…," New Orleans *Picayune*, 25 May 1861, 1; "The Seizures of Boats," Richmond [Va.] *Enquirer*, 31 May 1861, 4; "Camp Defiance Intelligence," New York *Herald*, 2 June 1861, 8, reprinting the Cairo [Ill.] *Camp Register* of 28 May; "River Intelligence," New Orleans *Delta*, 5 Nov 1861, 4; Memphis *Appeal*, 18 Dec 1861, 1: "River News and Steamboat Business" and "Compliment to the Alonzo Child"; "River Intelligence," Memphis *Public Ledger*, 6 Sept 1876, 4).

The North and South both needed pilots, and they too might be seized; but there is no evidence that Clemens piloted for either the United States or the Confederacy. Recalling this period in *Life on the Mississippi* (1883), he would express "curiosity" about the lot of the gunboat pilot "in his maiden battle, perched all solitary and alone on high in a pilot house, a target for Tom, Dick and Harry"; but in 1861 he was not so curious, being (according to his biographer, Albert Bigelow Paine) disinclined "to get up into a glass perch and be shot at by either side."[24] What evidence there is suggests that, in the opening days of the Civil War, Clemens's plan was to hide out in his family's St. Louis home and become a Freemason. In the closing days of 1860, Clemens had petitioned for membership in Polar Star Lodge No. 79, in St. Louis, and on 22 May 1861 he presented himself there for initiation. He would be at the lodge two more times in the next several weeks, making rapid progress through the degrees of that mystery. Freemasonry was popular among steamboatmen, and Clemens had a lifelong fascination with clubs, secret societies, initiations, and uniforms.[25]

24. SLC 1883, 281–82; *MTB*, 1:161.
25. Denslow 1924, 56; Jones 1954. Freemasons in Clemens's steamboating circle included captains John N. Bofinger, David DeHaven, and John A. Stevenson, and pilot Tom Moore (6 July 1859 to John T. Moore, *L1*, 91–93; 26 Dec 1860 to Polar Star Lodge No. 79, *L1*, 106–7 nn. 1–2; "Steamboat Calendar: Clemens's Piloting Assignments, 1857–1861," *L1*, 385–90; Grand Lodge of Missouri 1869, Appendix, 332; "River Intelligence," Memphis *Public Ledger*, 6 Sept 1876, 4; "Captain John A. Stevenson. Death of a Prominent Citizen and Leading Mason," New Orleans *Picayune*, 5 Apr 1901, 7). Clemens would resign from his lodge in 1869. When invited to a Masonic gathering in 1902 he reportedly said, in substance, that he had "got over all such foolishness" (Eutsey 2018).

Annie Moffett, Clemens's niece. Vassar College Library.

Clemens's St. Louis residence was the home of his sister, Pamela, her husband, William A. Moffett, their son, Samuel, and their daughter, Annie Moffett (later Webster, 1852–1930). We do not know where Clemens was on Friday, 10 May, when several regiments of Home Guards—Union volunteers, under the command of Captain Nathaniel Lyon—moved against Camp Jackson, an encampment of state militia near the federal arsenal in the western part of the city. Annie, eight years old at the time, was present in St. Louis and recalled the events many years later:

I remember very distinctly the 10th of May 1861, the day Camp Jackson was taken by General Lyon and his German Home Guard.

The young men of the city were camped there for their annual drill, but General Lyon was convinced that there was communication with the enemy and that there was to be an attempt to get arms to the South. He marched out, captured the camp and took the men prisoners. They were marched through the streets guarded by the Home Guards. A young man living opposite us had escaped; he went to the corner of Chestnut and 14th Streets to see them pass, foolishly wearing his cap. He was arrested and taken into the ranks. Our next neighbor, Mrs. Coleman, picked up a rock to throw at the Guard. Fortunately Mr. Schroeter caught her hand and stopped her, thus undoubtedly preventing bloodshed.

Two days later John Ladd stood on the steps of Dr. Brooks' church and deliberately fired into this same Guard. There was a panic, the members of the Home Guard thought the citizens were rising against them. They started to run, firing into the crowd and even the houses, several persons were killed and wounded, the excitement was intense.[26]

26. Webster 1918, 20–21.

In the wake of the violence in St. Louis, the Military Bill, which had languished before the state legislature, was quickly passed, reconstituting the old militia as the Missouri State Guard. Officially, the new force was pledged to defend Missouri against "all her enemies or opposers whatsoever"; in fact, it had been created for the specific purpose of resisting United States troops and ensuring Missouri's secession.[27] The State Guard's oath pledged allegiance to the state and the governor only, avoiding all mention of the United States and the Constitution. The federal government recognized it as a rebel army from the very first: General William S. Harney, the military commander at St. Louis, proclaimed on 14 May that the bill, now the Military Act, was "an indirect secession ordinance" and that the State Guard was one of the "unlawful combinations of men" that the United States Army was bound to suppress.[28]

Clemens was in St. Louis at this time. Annie Moffett remembered him hiding out in the family home, "obsessed with the fear that he might be arrested by government agents and forced to act as pilot on a government gunboat while a man stood by with a pistol ready to shoot him if he showed the least sign of a false move."[29] An incident related by Absalom C. Grimes, who

27. The 1861 Military Act is quoted from the abridged reprinting in U.S. Senate 1902 (253); the complete text is reprinted in the less widely available Missouri General Assembly 2001. For the publication and distribution of the Act, see U.S. Senate 1902, 255.

28. *OR*, 3:371–72.

29. *MTBus*, 60. The records of Polar Star Lodge No. 79 show that Clemens was present in St. Louis on 12 June (Denslow 1924, 56). His fear of being pressed into piloting service was not without foundation,

"Corner Scene during the Excitement at St. Louis, Missouri."
By M. Hastings, *Harper's Weekly*, 1 June 1861, 349.

would soon join Clemens's unit of the Missouri State Guard, is
suggestive in this connection.[30] Grimes wrote that in May 1861

---

as is clear from the history of Sam Bowen's capture, imprisonment, and
subsequent employment as an unwilling Union pilot. For Sam Bowen,
fictionalized in "The Private History" as Jo Bowers, see pp. 118–20, note
on 84.12.

30. Grimes's memoirs are indispensable to the study of "The Private
History." The most important of these, published in 1886, is discussed
below (pp. 30–34) and reprinted as Appendix B in this volume. For
Grimes, see pp. 125–26, note on 106.24.

he went to the steamboat inspector's office in St. Louis to renew his pilot's license. Here he learned from a German-born inspector that pilots were now required to swear allegiance to the United States; Grimes was willing to take the oath, but he would not have it administered by "an alien." Leaving the office, he met with Clemens and his fellow pilot Sam Bowen, and the three repaired to Hannibal, where federal soldiers soon arrested them and took them to St. Louis. At military headquarters, General John B. Gray threatened them with Union service, namely taking "a lot of boats (carrying soldiers) up to Boonville, on the Missouri River" in "the latter part of this week." They begged off, on the grounds that they were not Missouri River pilots, then fled when an opportunity presented itself.[31] Nowhere does Clemens mention anything like this, but there is nothing implausible about it, and Grimes's circumstantial details are compelling.

On 11 June, Governor Jackson, accompanied by Sterling Price (a former Missouri governor who now commanded the State Guard), met with Nathaniel Lyon (now a brigadier general

---

31. In the summer of 1861, John Burritt Gray (1831–96) was organizing Union volunteers in the St. Louis area. Grimes refers to him by his later title: he would not be adjutant general of Missouri until August 1862. Grimes implies that Gray is organizing for the battle of Boonville, which would place this interview before 13 June, when Missouri River steamboats carrying Union volunteers left St. Louis in pursuit of the governor's forces. Grimes writes that, after being captured in September 1862, he was condemned to death by a military commission headed by General Gray (Grimes 1879; Grimes 1926, 2–5, 88–89; Raymond 1887, 26–27; "From St. Louis," Cleveland *Leader*, 14 June 1861, 2; St. Louis *Missouri Democrat*: "General Orders No. 4," 7 Dec 1861, 2; "Special Orders, No. 256," 23 Aug 1862, 1).

Sam Bowen, ca. 1860. Mark Twain Boyhood Home and Museum, Hannibal.

commanding the Department of the West) and other Union leaders at the Planter's House in St. Louis. Negotiations broke down, and Jackson withdrew to Jefferson City, where on 12 June he issued a proclamation calling for fifty thousand state troops to repel the "invasion" of the state by the United States Army. "All our efforts toward conciliation have failed," wrote Jackson. "We can hope nothing from the justice or moderation of the agents of the Federal Government in this State....Rise, then, and drive out ignominiously the invaders who have dared to desecrate the soil which your labors have made fruitful and which is consecrated by your homes!"[32] On the same day, General Price directed his district commanders to assemble their troops for active service. Northeastern Missouri was in the second district, under the command of Clemens's "townsman," Thomas A. Harris, already mentioned as the author of the Military Bill.

Annie Moffett recalled a notable visit paid to Clemens while he was living quietly with her family:

> One day a man asked for Mr. Clemens and gave the name "Smith." Grandma went in and found one of Uncle Sam's friends. He had come with the wild project of forming a company to join General Price.
>
> Uncle Sam, tired of his life of inaction and the role of semi-prisoner, joyously agreed to the plan, and thus came his three weeks' experience as a Confederate soldier.[33]

32. *OR*, 53:696–98 (proclamation of 12 June 1861); Snead 1886, 198–201.

33. Webster 1918, 17. This is one of several passages from Annie Moffett Webster's "Family Chronicle" that appear in a rewritten state in *Mark*

A trio of Missouri Confederates. Clockwise from upper left: Claiborne Fox Jackson, ca. 1861; Sterling Price, ca. 1850; Thomas A. Harris. Photographs from the American Civil War Museum, Richmond, Virginia; illustration from the Louisville *Courier-Journal*, 10 April 1895, 7.

In "The Private History" Mark Twain places the formation of his entire company in Hannibal, but his notes made in 1877 and 1882 suggest that only Sam Bowen, Ed Stevens, and himself walked the gravel road from Hannibal to New London, in Ralls County, joining other recruits there.[34] In "The Private History" (and nowhere else) he calls the company the Marion Rangers, but he disguises many names; Grimes calls them the Ralls County Rangers, which, reflecting as it does the place of their enlistment and most of their activity, is likely the historical name. None of the men had any military training, and they brought what weapons they could. They were provided with mounts by Ralls County farmers, Clemens receiving a "very small mule," which, "on account of the close resemblance of the mule's tail to a paint brush," he named Paint-Brush.[35] As for uniforms, Missouri's

Twain, Business Man (1946), edited by her son, Samuel Charles Webster; how much of the rewriting is by Samuel is uncertain (e.g., compare with this passage *MTBus*, 60).

34. See Mark Twain's working notes for "Autobiography of a Damned Fool," quoted on p. 43; and *N&J2*, 486. Grimes writes that the group first formed up at Nuck Matson's house, near New London in Ralls County, and that the election of officers was at Goodwin's Mill, which was on Salt River about a mile and a half northeast of Cincinnati, Missouri (Briggs and Flowerree 1939, 140).

35. Grimes 1886 (Appendix B, p. 137); Grimes 1926, 6. Writing from Nevada in January 1862, Clemens responded to the news that his mule had passed into Union service: " 'Paint-Brush' in the hands of the enemy! God forgive me! this is the first time I have felt melancholy since I left the United States. And he is doing service for the enemy. But *against his will.*...However, if he has gone over to the enemy, let him go. He can't be depended on anyhow—he'll desert at the first opportunity; if he don't fall in a camp-kettle and get drowned" (OC and SLC to MEC, 29, 30, and 31 Jan 1862, *L1*, 143–45).

Military Board had not had time to design or manufacture any; until it did, General Price recommended that "companies now forming…adopt a gray flannel shirt, gray pantaloons, and felt hat."[36]

In 1902 Clemens would tentatively date his departure from Hannibal "in the second week of June, 1861."[37] As a Mississippi River port and the eastern terminus of Missouri's major railroad, Hannibal was busy with Union troops, coming in from Illinois and Iowa and passing into the interior of the state.[38] Clemens may be the "SAM" who wrote the following dispatch from Union-occupied Hannibal. It was published on 18 June in the St. Louis *Missouri State Journal*. This recently founded secessionist paper had close ties to Governor Jackson. Its editor, J. W. Tucker, had just been arrested for treason, and the *State Journal* itself would soon be suppressed by the Union army:

To the Editor of the Daily Mo. State Journal:
   Four of the Home Guards deserted Saturday night, and left for parts unknown. I heard from a very reliable source that there were seventeen bodies sent up the river this morning killed in a skirmish up the railroad somewhere. It is not known where, for the

36. Orders dated 1 June (Price 1861).
37. "Affection of Old Friends Moves Mark Twain to Tears," St. Louis *Republic*, 31 May 1902, 1.
38. "Movement of Troops," St. Louis *Missouri Democrat*, 15 June 1861, 2, reprinting the Quincy (Ill.) *Whig* of 13 June; Davenport (Iowa) *Quad-City Times*: "Iowa Troops Ordered to Hannibal," 15 June 1861, 1; "Removal of the Troops from Hannibal," 18 June 1861, 1.

wires were cut down. I know, myself, that they sent for the 400 soldiers that were left here, *in a hurry*, Friday afternoon. There are about 250 Home Guards here at present, and there is a requisition from General Scott here, for the troops that have been sent here. I don't know what the Home Guards will do when they go away, but they are scared bad enough now.

The boys are responding bravely to the call of the Governor—about fifty have left already, and plenty left to strike when the proper time comes. Major T. A. Harris received his commission Friday night, (per courier) and has left for the seat of war. He is Brigadier-General for this district. Our city is perfectly quiet at present.

Yours, in haste,

SAM.[39]

39. From internal evidence the dispatch seems to have been written on 16 June 1861. As no copy of the *State Journal* containing the dispatch has been located, the text given here is reconstructed from two contemporary reprints: "From Hannibal," Louisville *Courier*, 20 June 1861, 1, and "Hannibal Correspondence," Hannibal *Messenger*, 20 June 1861, 2. The dispatch refers to events "up the railroad," i.e., the Hannibal and St. Joseph Railroad, which traversed the state from the Mississippi to the Kansas border; to General Winfield Scott (1786–1866), the venerable commanding general of the United States Army; and to the State Guard Brigadier General Thomas A. Harris. The reprint in the Hannibal *Messenger* adds editorial comments criticizing "Sam's" loyalty, veracity, and diction (reprinted in Lorch 1941, 467 n. 46). On the *Missouri State Journal*, see Peckham 1866, 286–89, and Rule 2002, but note that both misdate Tucker's arrest, which was on 14 June, preceding the suppression of the *Journal* by almost a month (St. Louis *Missouri Democrat*: "The Editor of the State Journal Arrested for Treason," 15 June 1861, 2; "Military Matters," 13 July 1861, 3).

This clumsily written dispatch is not easy to attribute to Clemens, even "in haste." The author could be almost any Sam from Hannibal—Sam Bowen, for example—but Clemens's confirmed journalistic tendencies tend to favor his authorship. A New Orleans fortune teller had recently told him: "You have written a great deal; you write well—but you are rather out of practice." It is true he had written little lately for publication, but his two most recent newspaper contributions had been signed, like this one, "SAM."[40]

In "The Private History" and elsewhere Clemens refers to his Missouri State Guard service as time spent in "the Confederate army" or "the rebel army." These claims may seem inaccurate; Missouri was not in the Confederacy, as much as some of its leaders and citizens hoped to see it there, and the State Guard had no constitutional affiliation to the Confederacy while Clemens was in its service. But since the State Guard was absorbed into the Confederate army in due course, and since it had always been "Southern" and secessionist in intention, few cared to split this hair. We might say that if the Missouri State Guard was not *the* rebel army, it was *a* rebel army.[41]

40. 6 Feb 1861 to OC and MEC, *L1*, 107–16; SLC 1859 (evidently intended for the St. Louis *Missouri Republican*); and SLC 1860. From my count of Clemens's "most recent newspaper contributions" I exclude two publications of pilot's memoranda, which were signed by Clemens and his co-pilot with full names, as convention dictated.

41. To judge from newspaper reports, in June and July 1861 the Missouri State Guard was called "rebel" but not "Confederate." On 31 October 1861 Claiborne Jackson's government-in-exile was admitted to the Confederacy,

Colonel John Ralls would have sworn Clemens's company into the State Guard according to its official oath; an act of the legislature had mandated the distribution of five thousand copies of the text of the Military Act for use in "the organization, government, and support" of State Guard units. The oath read:

"You, each and every one of you, do solemnly swear, or affirm (as the case may be), that you will bear true allegiance to the State of Missouri, and that you will serve her honestly and faithfully against all her enemies or opposers whatsoever; that you will support the constitution of the State of Missouri and observe and obey the orders of the governor of Missouri, and the orders of the officers appointed over you, whilst on duty, according to the rules and articles for the government of the Missouri State Guard; so help you God."[42]

---

and control of the State Guard was transferred to Jefferson Davis; from that date it could certainly be seen as "officially" Confederate. By that time Clemens, of course, was long gone (*OR*, 53:753–55; "The Boonville Battle—Particulars of the Defeat of the Missourians," Cincinnati *Press*, 20 June 1861, 2; "From Cairo," St. Louis *Missouri Democrat*, 28 June 1861, 2; and Hannibal *Messenger*: "Arrest of W. B. Thompson," 19 Sept 1861, 3; "The Elite of the Rebel Army," 2 Oct 1861, 2; "Editorial Correspondence," 5 Nov 1861, 2; "The Price–Halleck Letters," 29 Jan 1862, 2). The question of whether the Missouri State Guard was a Confederate army was taken up by the United States Bureau of Pensions in 1896. Aaron T. Bush, who had served in the State Guard from July through December 1861, was denied a military pension "on account of service in the Confederate army." Bush appealed the decision, testifying that "if it [the State Guard] was a Confederate service he did not intend it as such," and stating that he had resigned when "Governor Jackson turned out to be a rebel." The bureau rejected Bush's appeal, citing Jackson's public proclamations and his battles against the United States as evidence that the State Guard should be considered "Confederate" (Hall and Bixler 1897, 254–56).

42. In Clemens's 1877 speech about the war, as reported in the Hartford

In "The Private History" Mark Twain says that the oath "mixed us considerably, and we could not make out just what service we were embarked in."[43] If by this Clemens means to plead ignorance of the State Guard's stance in the incipient Civil War, that is hardly plausible. Governor Jackson's Southern and secessionist drift was more than apparent in the call for volunteers Clemens says he was answering; Absalom Grimes, for one, seems to have understood that he and his companions were "recruits for the rebel army...assembled in behalf of the South."[44] But it is true that Missouri's unprecedented situation was fraught with conceptual difficulties. Clemens may well have wondered whether his oath to "drive all invaders from her soil" might oblige him to fight a "friendly" invasion by armies of the Southern Confederacy; Governor Jackson was known to be inviting such aid. Another perplexity was to be found in Jackson's proclamation of 12 June, which instructed Missourians that they were bound to obey the "constitutional requirements of the Federal Government" but not the "unconstitutional edicts of the military despotism which has enthroned itself at Washington"![45]

No official record attests to the service, or even the existence, of the Ralls County Rangers, under that name or any other. All our

Courant, allegiance to the Constitution is specified (SLC 1877 [Appendix A, p. 130]).

43. This claim substantially repeats his 1877 speech: "We couldn't really tell which side we were on, but we went into camp and left it to the God of Battles, (for that was the term then)" (SLC 1877 [Appendix A, p. 130]).

44. Appendix B, p. 136.

45. "Gov. Jackson, of Missouri, to Be Caught and Hung," New York _Times_, 16 June 1861, 4; _OR_, 53:698.

information comes from unofficial accounts, namely Clemens's writings and speeches, and the various memoirs of Absalom Grimes.[46] Grimes (1834–1911), born in Kentucky and raised in Missouri, had been a steamboat pilot on the upper Mississippi since the age of sixteen. His sympathies were Southern, and after his stint in the State Guard he would gain fame as a Confederate spy and mail runner, repeatedly captured and escaped. His memoir, published in 1926 as *Absalom Grimes, Confederate Mail Runner,* is the fruit of a late-in-life collaboration with his adult daughter, Charlotte Mitchell, as edited after Grimes's death by historian M. M. Quaife.

Grimes was an erratic and turbulent individual, but he had the sharp eye and retentive memory that make a good pilot—or spy. It is true, as John Gerber wrote, that *Confederate Mail Runner* sometimes reads "more like old Southwestern yarn-spinning than history"; but where it is possible to test Grimes's accuracy, research generally vindicates him.[47] Grimes uses real names where Clemens often disguises them; and where Clemens alters facts for personal, professional, and artistic reasons, Grimes has no such scruples. Grimes's daughter dated the composition of *Confederate Mail Runner* to "the spring of 1910 and 1911," pointing to its basis in her father's wartime diaries; but it is now clear that the book

46. Paine's account of the Ralls County Rangers draws upon "The Private History" and upon some version of Grimes's memoir as well (*MTB*, 1:163–69).

47. Gerber 1955, 38. Gerber's article is compromised by his ascription to Clemens of the "Quintus Curtius Snodgrass" letters, which was later conclusively debunked (Bates 1964).

Salt River, near Florida, Missouri. Photograph by Albert Bigelow Paine, 1907. Mark Twain Papers.

revises material that Grimes had written decades earlier. Much of this early material has been found in newspapers, where an autobiographical chunk will appear as an interview or a letter to the editor.[48] As valuable as it has been to Mark Twain scholarship, the chapter of *Confederate Mail Runner* that deals with the Ralls County Rangers is now secondary in importance to an earlier version. Recently discovered in the St. Louis *Missouri Republican* ("A Staunch Democratic Journal"), it is explicitly a rejoinder to Mark Twain's *Century* article:

48. Grimes 1876, 1877, 1879, 1886.

I see in the December number of the New York *Century*, Mark, himself, has endeavored to give a "Private History" of a "Campaign That Failed," but in doing so I consider his memory sadly at fault, and very many interesting events of his war history have been omitted, and other events he has not accurately described, according to my recollection.

Grimes's 1886 article, unmediated by amanuenses, contains elements which help to focus the historical status of Mark Twain's story, and which were refined away in *Confederate Mail Runner*. In particular it sheds light on the feature of "The Private History" most frequently singled out as a fiction: the killing of the unarmed stranger. Evidence that the episode is invented is seldom cited, but several considerations cast doubt upon it: it is not mentioned by Mark Twain in any writing, public or private, before his 1885 article, and, except for one speech delivered in 1887, it is never mentioned again; and Mark Twain's "war paper" was originally to be highly fictionalized, even to the point of including Huck, Tom, and Jim, a detail that encourages the idea that fictional elements persist in the final text.[49] But the decisive contribution comes from Grimes, who, in two sentences present only in the 1886 article, expressly states that the homicide is Mark Twain's embroidery of a real event. The two sentences are italicized here:

49. The speech referred to is SLC 1887. For Mark Twain's early notes toward his war paper, see pp. 43–44.

Absalom Grimes, ca. 1863.
Courtesy of Yale University Press.

Mark Twain refers to a "man that was killed in camp one night," the circumstances are these: One dark, rainy night (I think the very next night after I fired on the mullen stalks), a good-natured fellow (but a hard case), by the name of Dave Young—who was always about three-thirds full of whiskey—was placed on camp guard. During the night many of us were awakened by heavy tramping and presently we heard the guard say "halt you! Ain't you going to halt and give the pass-word?" The tramping still continued, which, with the order of the guard, had aroused a good many of the boys, when the guard cried again: "Halt or I'll shoot," and bang, bang went both barrels of his gun. A heavy fall and a groan, and up and out into the dark all hands rushed, and to the place from whence proceded the groans, and there lay in the agonies of death an old gray horse, the property of Dave Young (the guard), himself, who was standing over him looking quite sad. *That was the only killing I ever knew of in that camp—or while Mark was in the army.*[50]

50. Grimes 1886 (Appendix B, p. 144).

While it is good to be able to add Grimes's testimony to the record, it remains true that if the killing is fictional it is, as Fred Lorch observed, "utterly without value as a reason why Mark Twain didn't do anything in the war, the explanation of which was his stated purpose in writing 'The Private History.'"[51]

Grimes also confirms the fictional nature of another element in Mark Twain's story. The recruit called Peterson d'Un Lap, a much-commented-on character with a place in Mark Twain's ongoing critique of "Southern" romanticism and artificiality, is based upon a historical individual, but the individual was not in the Ralls County Rangers or any other unit. D'Un Lap owes his presence in the tale to an event of March 1885, when Clemens received a letter from the Hannibal schoolmate he had known as John L. Robards. Observing that his correspondent was now spelling his name "RoBards," Clemens wrote on the envelope: "This was always a poor well meaning ass—& at last has gone & stuck that big B in the middle of his name!"[52] At that moment, Clemens had just recently undertaken to write a war memoir, and RoBards was just the man to skewer as a victim of Southern vanity and artificiality—what Mark Twain called "the Walter Scott disease."[53] The fact that d'Un Lap is recognizably based on RoBards has led to the mistaken conclusion that RoBards was a member of the Ralls County Rangers; the evidence is against this. Writing of his friendship with Mark Twain,

51. Lorch 1941, 456.
52. RoBards to SLC, 24 Mar 1885, CU-MARK.
53. *Life on the Mississippi*, chaps. 40, 45, and 46, in which last the quoted phrase occurs.

RoBards mentions Clemens's enlistment as "a Lieutenant in the Confederate army, under General Thomas Harris," but makes no such claim for himself; and RoBards's entry in a Missouri biographical compendium, undoubtedly written by himself, enumerates his brothers' services in the war, again claiming none for himself. The injury that prevented him from attending West Point and excused him from military service, together with the fact that in June 1861 he was a young lawyer who had just opened a practice in Hannibal, weigh against his participation, and the fact that RoBards is unknown to Grimes confirms that his presence in "The Private History" is a fiction born entirely of Clemens's impulse to satirize his pretentious friend.[54]

A volunteer's term of service in the Missouri State Guard was seven years. By his own account, Clemens managed two weeks.[55] Grimes says the company disbanded at the home of Enoch G. "Nuck" Matson, near New London, and that Clemens had a sprained ankle that kept him laid up there while the other recruits drifted away.[56] In *Life on the Mississippi* Clemens says that when he "retired from the rebel army" in 1861 he retired "in good order" upon the town of Louisiana, in Pike County,

54. RoBards 1915, 164; Stevens 1915, 4:265; *Inds*, 345–46.
55. The seven-year term is stated in the Military Act, and in Sterling Price's orders of 1 June 1861. Troops who had been in the field for six months, however, had the option of either re-volunteering or going home (U.S. Senate 1902, 252; Price 1861). For Clemens's "two weeks" of soldiering, see pp. 40, 43, and 72; also SLC 1887, SLC 1897, 679–80, and *AutoMT3*, 490, note on 100.30–32.
56. Grimes 1886 (Appendix B, pp. 149–50). For Matson (Mark Twain's "Farmer Mason"), see p. 121, note on 88.10.

Missouri.[57] From Matson's farm he could have gone by road from New London to Louisiana, disposed of Paint-Brush, and taken a steamboat to St. Louis, where the diary of Orion's wife, Mollie Clemens, places him in the first days of July.[58]

If Clemens had been arrested as an armed belligerent, what punishment lay in store for him? Conjectural answers to this question have spiced biographies, quoting the terms of military proclamations that were made long after his departure. Clemens's war was so brief that only a single proclamation is pertinent: on 18 June, General Lyon proclaimed that Missourians who "have taken up arms, or who are now preparing to do so," were "invited to return to their homes, and relinquish their hostile attitude to the General Government, and are assured that they may do so without being molested for past occurrences."[59] Later on, the emergence of violent bands of bushwhackers would cause the Union forces to decree harsher terms; but it seems Clemens, who laid down his arms in July 1861, was in the clear.[60]

57. SLC 1883, 523.

58. Mollie records that Orion left Keokuk for St. Louis on 4 July, a trip that usually took something over sixteen hours, and implies that he met Samuel on arrival in St. Louis. Clemens was certainly in St. Louis by 10 July, when he was present at Polar Star Lodge No. 79 to be raised to the Sublime Degree of Master Mason. Paine's statement that Clemens made a trip to Keokuk derives from Grimes, who merely supposes: "I believe he went to Keokuk and went to California with his brother"; Orion's home at this time was not Keokuk but Memphis, Missouri (Grimes 1886 [Appendix B, p. 151]; MEC 1862, 10–11; SLC 1883, 203; Denslow 1924, 56; *MTB*, 1:168).

59. Peckham 1866, 275.

60. The history of Sam Bowen does not support the idea that the former

"The Private History" has Clemens's company dispersing after hearing of the approach of a Union army, under the command of a colonel who would later prove to be Ulysses S. Grant. This piece of wishful thinking is based upon a discovery made by Clemens in 1885, in the process of publishing Grant's *Personal Memoirs*. Clemens visited the ailing Grant in New York on 26 May 1885, recording in his notebook: "To-day talked with General Grant about his & my first Missouri campaign in 1861 (in June or July.) He surprised an empty camp near Florida, Mo., on Salt river, which I had been occupying a day or two before. How near he came to playing the devil with his future publisher!"[61] In "The Private History" Mark Twain goes further,

---

Ralls County Rangers were "liable to be shot on sight," as has been claimed (for example, Scharnhorst 2018, 132–33). On 24 February 1862 Bowen was arrested in Hannibal by soldiers of the 21st Missouri infantry brigade under Colonel David Moore, which was stationed in Hannibal from 20 February to 19 March 1862. By this time Missouri was under martial law, but Bowen was not shot. He was treated according to the most recent general order of the military command at St. Louis: rebels were to be arrested, and they would be unconditionally released on taking an oath of allegiance, unless they had violated "the laws of war" or were "notoriously bad and dangerous men." Bowen refused the oath and was imprisoned. Within a month or so he took the oath and was soon piloting a Union transport (Hannibal *Messenger*: "Arrival of Col. Moore's Regiment," 21 Feb 1862, 3; "Gen. Halleck's Circular," 22 Feb 1862, 2; "The Oath of Allegiance," 25 Feb 1862, 3; "Departure of the 21st from St. Louis," 22 Mar 1862, 3).

61. *N&J3*, 153. In May 1885 Clemens was reading proofs of the *Memoirs'* first volume, in which Grant tells of his expedition in pursuit of Tom Harris. The interest of the passage was certainly noted by someone at Charles L. Webster and Company, who used it in making up the salesman's prospectus—the "dummy" book used in canvassing subscriptions, printed

saying that he "came within a few hours" of confronting Grant's army when it marched on Thomas A. Harris's camp. But Grant set out for, and arrived at, this camp on 17 July 1861, and on that date Clemens was in St. Louis, about to embark for St. Joseph and the overland route to Nevada.[62] His brother, Orion Clemens (1825–97), had campaigned for Lincoln, and the new president now appointed him secretary of Nevada Territory. The post was second in command to the governor, and allowed Orion to offer his brother the unofficial post of secretary-to-the-secretary. The war was expected to be brief, and Clemens had no thought of bidding a final farewell to piloting when he "started across the plains to be gone 3 months & have the recreation we all needed (thinking the war would be closed & the river open again by that time)." With Orion, he left St. Louis on 18 July, three days before the first battle of Bull Run. He could not know there would be four more years of civil war, compared with which the war he left behind was mere skirmishing.[63]

around May (Grant 1885–86, 1:248–51; salesman's prospectus, 261, CU-MARK; Apr 1885 to Webster, NPV; Webster to SLC, 22 Apr 1885, CU-MARK).

62. Grant 1969, 72 n. 2; Lorch 1941, 463. Grant was actually the second Union colonel to march on Harris's camp in Florida, Missouri. Between 8 and 11 July, Colonel Robert F. Smith and seven companies of infantry set out from Palmyra for the camp, only to be ambushed and surrounded by Harris's men (*OR*, 3:40–41; Grant 1969, 69). For Clemens's whereabouts during this time, see note 58 (p. 36).

63. 25 Aug 1866 to Will Bowen, *L1*, 357–60; MEC 1862, 11.

2. "I will invent a few warlike passages"

Over many years, Clemens became visibly "reconstructed." By 1864 his journalism written in San Francisco was treating the cause of the South as unworthy.[64] In 1870 he married into a staunch abolitionist family, and settled happily among the Yankees of Hartford. He spoke at Union Army gatherings, campaigned (exclusively, if we except a Mugwump crisis in 1884) for the Republican Party, and published the memoirs of the Union generals Grant, McClellan, Sheridan, and Sherman. We do not find him repudiating his old rebel friends, who seem mostly to have continued in their Southern sympathies.[65] He had stern words for the South and "Southern ideas," and he rejected the idea of racial inferiority—citing, to be sure, the races' equal depravity: "All that I care to know is that a man is a human being—that is enough for me; he can't be any worse."[66]

For almost a decade Clemens preserved public silence about his part in the war. The first crack in the facade opened when

64. See, for example, the articles collected in *CofC*, 263–78.

65. Will Bowen's 10 December 1889 letter to Clemens, quoted for its biographical details on p. 5, is mostly a eulogy of the recently deceased Jefferson Davis. Bowen projects his admiration right into the bosom of Clemens's own family: "Firmly I believe those little Yankee girls of yours will teach their little ones, to link his name reverently with Washington Lincoln & Lee[.] Great Americans! The question of State Right^s is on trial, & on the verdict depends the future of our Boys & Girls—The Liberties of the people....History will write Jeff Davis the Saviour perhaps—but at least the apostle of Liberty to Americans" (CU-MARK).

66. SLC 1899, 528. The phrase "Southern ideas" is quoted from *Life on the Mississippi*, chap. 40 (SLC 1883, 419).

a letter from Clemens to M. Jeff Thompson was leaked to the press. In civilian life, Thompson (1826–76) was an engineer and a prominent citizen of St. Joseph, Missouri. At the outbreak of war, Claiborne Jackson commissioned him a brigadier general in the State Guard, after which service he won fame as a bushwhacker in Missouri and Arkansas. In 1874 Thompson was pleased to find that Mark Twain and Charles Dudley Warner had used him as a character in their novel *The Gilded Age*. A triangular correspondence ensued, and Thompson leaked the letter he received from Clemens. The New Orleans *Republican* printed it on 19 April 1874, noting that it was "not intended for publication."[67] Addressing Thompson as "My Dear General," Clemens struck a tone of old-soldier bonhomie, somewhat improved by the frank admission that it was unearned:

> Warner tells me to write you, and says he has just written. I have no news that you would care to hear, because, although I was a soldier in the rebel army in Missouri for two weeks once, we never won any victories to speak of. We never could get the enemy to stay still when we wanted to fight, and we were generally on the move when the enemy wanted to fight. Our campaign is not even referred to in the shabby record which they call "history." But historians are almighty mean people, any way.
>
> However, if you will drop in here and let this roof shelter you awhile I will invent a few warlike passages that ought to content a

67. This letter was included in *L6*, 96–100, where it was edited from a reprint; the differences between *L6* and the original publication, which is followed here, are few ("Letter from Mark Twain," New Orleans *Republican*, 19 Apr 1874, 8).

soldier. Warner the Peaceful is my next door neighbor. Warner has never been to war, and so he is a trifle dull in his experiences, but he means well. Come and you shall be introduced to him.

Yours truly,

SAMUEL L. CLEMENS.

This letter was reprinted and excerpted in papers both Northern and Southern. All noted that Mark Twain had been a "rebel" or "Confederate"; several formed the mistaken impression that he had served under M. Jeff Thompson; none registered any indignation.

The same was the case early in 1876 when Absalom Grimes was interviewed on the subject of Mark Twain's "experiences as a Confederate officer." The main features of Grimes's narrative were already in place, and his story would remain consistent through years of further interviewing.[68] In January 1877 an excerpt from another article about Grimes was much circulated:

In June, 1861, in company with Samuel Clemens and Samuel Bowen, all river pilots, I joined the Ralls County Rangers of the Missouri State Militia under Gen. Tom Harris. We were put into camp near Florida, in Ralls County, without tents, arms or commissary stores. We soon broke camp. Clemens started out West to California, and turned humorist under the nom de plume of

68. Grimes 1876. A newspaper item published shortly afterward said: "Mark Twain acknowledges that he has only one thing against himself, and that is that he once served three weeks as Second Lieutenant in the rebel army, and rode a confederate mule" (Leavenworth [Kan.] *Times*, 20 Feb 1876, 6). If this was an actual statement by Clemens, rather than an extrapolation from Grimes, it has not been found.

"Mark Twain." Sam Bowen was captured at Hannibal and joined the Saw-horse cavalry, being detailed to saw wood for the Federal Colonel, David Moore. I went to Paris, Monroe County, where I joined a company under Col. Brace; then fell under command of Martin E. Green.[69]

The implications of Grimes's facts were developed by the New York *World* in an item that was picked up by papers nationwide: "Has Mark Twain taken the iron-clad oath, or is he an unreconstructed rebel?…We are loath to believe that Mr. Twain ever lifted a fratricidal hand against Gen. Joe Hawley."[70] Grimes would continue to recount his exploits, and Clemens's, for the newspapers.[71] Grimes's information was remembered by a local historian, Return I. Holcombe, who in 1883 was pestering Clemens for information for his forthcoming *History of Marion County, Missouri*. On 24 September Holcombe asked about an article that "went the rounds some time ago, giving a very improbable account of your experience as a rebel soldier. I wish to ask if there is *any* truth to it? *Did* you really go out awhile under Tom Harris and Mart. Green? If you didn't, you

69. Grimes 1877. For Sam Bowen's wartime history, see note 60 (pp. 36–37).

70. Untitled item, New York *World*, 25 Jan 1877, 4. Joseph R. Hawley (1826–1905) served as governor of Connecticut and as a Republican congressman from that state; he was also a Union veteran with a distinguished battle record, an editor and owner of the Hartford *Courant*, Clemens's political ally, and a Hartford neighbor. Clemens had lately campaigned for Hawley in his 1876 bid for re-election to Congress (Cohn 2015).

71. Grimes 1879; Grimes 1886 (Appendix B).

probably stood alone at one time among the entire adult white male population of Marion County, for everybody here in '61 seems to have been 'Southern.'" On the envelope Clemens wrote: "D—n this everlasting man."[72]

Whether or not he was prompted by Grimes's revelations, Clemens would make 1877 the year he went public with his war history. In the holdings of the Mark Twain Papers, housed within The Bancroft Library at the University of California, Berkeley, are three leaves of manuscript notes about his Missouri campaign. These were, until recently, cataloged as notes for "The Private History of a Campaign That Failed," but the pagination, stationery, and internal evidence combine to show that they are notes toward the untitled manuscript known as "Autobiography of a Damned Fool."[73] This work was begun in March 1877 and probably abandoned within weeks. It was supposed to chronicle the life and vagaries of a character named Bolivar, principally based on Orion, but the notes show that Clemens planned to invest the character with his own—and especially Sam Bowen's—wartime experiences:

> 2 weeks campaign (umbrellas) with Ed Stevens & Sam Bowen.
> "What you lack (to Bowen) is stability of character."
> Horse used to bite Sam's legs while he was asleep.
> Complained of the villainy of having picket guards rainy nights, when no enemy but a dam fool would venture out.

72. Holcombe to SLC, 24 Sept 1883, CU-MARK. Holcombe's published account of Clemens's war record is Holcombe 1884, 931–32.
73. MS in CU-MARK; published in S&B, 134–64.

Cut loose from Tom Harris & all other authority to have their own way.

Ab Grimes.

The old man with the huge cleaver.

Sam took mosquito blisters for a mortal disease.

Used to sit on his horse in prairie on picket duty & cry & curse & go to sleep in hot sun.

Sent our washing to town because didn't like country washing.

Mule scraped me off going in at stable; Ed's horse did the same for him on a knot of an oak.

Beginning.—In June '61, Bol. was in St Louis; Claib Jackson called for 50,000 militia to "repel invasion." Bol went to Han & raised 2 recruits—walked to N. London in night. Received a sword—marched to Col. Ralls & had his Co sworn in. Bowen called it a batallion—then a reg't then a brigade—then a Division—then a corps. Enormous liar & braggart.

Rats would bite his feet when asleep in corn crib & he would think it snakes & cry & curse.

Used to curse me, his superior, & I threatened court martial & death.

The extant manuscript of "Autobiography of a Damned Fool" does not draw on these notes; perhaps the material was too precious to be frittered away on Orion. The same fund of anecdote, however, is visible in the speech Clemens gave later that year, on 2 October 1877, at a Hartford banquet given by a local social organization, the Putnam Phalanx, in honor of the visiting Ancient and Honorable Artillery Company of Massachusetts. It was here that he inaugurated the public history of his private history. His speech, which is reprinted as Appendix A, drew upon his notes made earlier in the year, and treated his experience of Missouri's Civil War as matter for farce. The speech, which was widely reprinted, did not forestall alternative accounts of Mark Twain's war.

The public statements of Horace E. Bixby confirm Mark Twain's assertion that steamboat pilots loved to "load up the confiding stranger with the most picturesque and admirable lies."[74] Mark Twain's *Atlantic Monthly* serial "Old Times on the Mississippi" publicized his mentor under the name of "Mr. B——" and Bixby was keen to return the favor.[75] In 1882 he gave a New Orleans paper this account of Clemens's war:

> When the war broke out Sam was standing pilot watch on the Alonzo Childs. When the line of division was made between the North and South the Childs was turned to the southward. Sam immediately became her pilot, and ran the river for a year. At the end of that time he came to Hannibal, Mo, his native place, and enlisted in the Confederate army as a private with Sterling Price.[76]

Bixby's sometime connection with Clemens entitled him to frequent interviewing, and he freely varied the terms of his tale, saying in one interview, for example, that Clemens piloted three months, rather than a year, for the Confederacy.[77] In any case, no period of one year, or six months, or even three months piloting in the seceded states will fit into Clemens's known movements after April 1861.

74. SLC 1883, 247.
75. SLC 1875a–e.
76. "Down the River," New Orleans *Picayune*, 25 Jan 1882, 9.
77. Interviews with Bixby are collected in Tenney 1998.

Clemens was aware of the liberties Bixby was taking with his personal history, but made no comment on it.[78] Indeed, he seems never to have repudiated *any* version of his wartime history. His chosen course was to state his case and refrain from answering charges. "I can't reply when the newspapers make misstatements about me," he wrote to a newspaper editor. "It wouldn't do— the public would quickly tire of it."[79] If he reasoned that his own statements would prove more interesting, more quotable, and therefore more durable than other people's, he was right. He did, however, comply with an invitation to deny, semi-publicly, another interesting claim. In March 1885 a professor at Kansas State University alerted Clemens to a rumor that placed him among "the famous, or infamous, Quantrill band," which had raided Lawrence, Kansas, in 1863. The professor sought permission to contradict this rumor, and received this reply from Clemens, which he leaked to the newspapers:

> It is always my policy to confess anything I was charged with, because this saves discussion—and I would rather commit six crimes than discuss one. But in this case I am debarred from confessing, for some meddler would be sure to crop up somewhere,

78. In her letter to Clemens of 2 Sept 1882, his aunt Ella Lampton enclosed a copy of the 1882 Bixby interview, as reprinted in the St. Louis *Post-Dispatch* (CU-MARK).

79. 6 July 1885 to Editor of the Boston *Herald*, CU-MARK. Compare the statement dictated by Clemens on 18 May 1885: "It is my settled policy to allow newspapers to make as many misstatements about me or my affairs as they like" ("Grant's Memoirs," *AutoMT1*, 93).

and convict me of lying for the sake of effect! Charge me with some other crime—then I'm your man.[80]

The situation, as Clemens construes it, is richly convoluted. Falsely accused, he wants to confess (and perjure himself), but is "debarred" by the "meddler" who will expose his innocence. The jest parallels his position as he set out, in 1885, to write his war memoir: telling the truth would show him up as embarrassingly innocuous, while fictionalizing will expose him as a liar. In "The Private History" he would divide Americans into those who "did something" in the war and those who "did nothing"—aware, no doubt, that the "something" he had done could be attacked as treason, and the "nothing" as cowardice or desertion. He was getting up into that glass perch where he might be shot at by either side.

3. "We want a Missouri guerrilla"

In November 1884 the *Century Magazine* began publication of a series of articles on "Battles and Leaders of the Civil War." This would consist of contributions by highly placed participants, commissioned in the belief that, twenty years after the end of the war, "new knowledge and the wisdom of cool reflection" promised to "soften controversy with that better understanding of each other, which comes to comrades in arms when personal

80. "Mark Twain a Member of the Quantrell Gang," Lawrence (Kans.) *Evening Tribune*, 16 Mar 1885, 1.

Samuel L. Clemens, 12 or 13 January 1885. Detail of a photograph taken by Wales McCormick at Quincy, Illinois. Mark Twain Papers.

feeling has dissipated."[81] By March 1885, "Battles and Leaders" had featured (among others) P. G. T. Beauregard on Bull Run, Lew Wallace on Fort Donelson, James B. Eads on the Mississippi River gunboats, and Ulysses S. Grant on Shiloh. Overseen by *Century* editors Robert Underwood Johnson and Clarence C. Buel, the series boosted the magazine's circulation from 127,000 to 225,000 copies, garnering an estimated reading audience of two million. Clemens was keeping a close eye on these figures, writing in his notebook on 26 February that Grant's article "had sprung their circulation clear away up into the clouds."[82]

The *Century* had been launched as recently as 1881, but Clemens was among those who recognized its preeminence as a magazine of general literature. From November 1884 through February 1885, the *Century* ran extracts from *Adventures of Huckleberry Finn* alongside the earliest papers in the "war

81. "Topics of the Time: Battles and Leaders of the Civil War," *Century Magazine* 28 (Oct 1884): 943–44.

82. Johnson and Buel 1887–89, "Preface," vol. 1, p. x; *N&J3*, 97.

series." At that point, however, author and magazine paused to smooth over a conflict. Ulysses S. Grant, in poverty and dying of throat cancer, was completing the composition of his memoirs. He had written three articles for the *Century* series, and there was an understanding that the magazine's parent Century Company was to publish the memoirs—until February, when Clemens persuaded Grant to publish with his own firm, Charles L. Webster and Company. The parties were coming to an arrangement, but there remained a sense that Clemens owed the Century Company, in Johnson's words, a "favor" that might "restore the balance somewhat, & put us in a devilish good humor."[83] In early March, Clemens visited the *Century* offices in Union Square to hash out some remaining differences over the Grant business, and Johnson sought to enlist him in the war series. He followed up with a letter: "I was not joking the other day in suggesting to you that you should write out your experiences in the Rebel Army.... Already we are roping into the Series the literary men of both sections, including Higginson and others of the Northern side, and Maurice Thompson, Cable and yourself among the eminent rebels."[84] Clemens's reply was enthusiastic: "The fact is, the War Series is the greatest thing of these modern times, & nobody who is anybody can well

83. Johnson to SLC, 10 Aug 1885, CU-MARK.
84. Johnson to SLC, 16 Mar 1885. Johnson mentions three contemporary writers who had served in the Civil War: Thomas Wentworth Higginson (1823–1911), James Maurice Thompson (1844–1901), and George Washington Cable (1844–1925), in whose company Clemens had recently completed a four-month lecture tour in the East, the Midwest, and Canada.

afford to be unrepresented in it"; but citing pressure of work, he put Johnson off until the summer.[85] Clemens's flattery had an object: the Century Company planned to collect the completed war papers as a multi-volume set, and he meant to poach that publication for his own firm, as he had done with the Grant memoirs. "Keep on good terms with the Century people," he wrote to Charles L. Webster, the titular head of his publishing company and husband of Clemens's niece. "We will presently prove to them that they can't *afford* to publish their war book themselves—we must have it."[86]

Flushed with the success of *Huckleberry Finn* and the acquisition of the extremely promising Grant book, Clemens was indeed more publisher than writer at the moment. His earliest notes toward his own war memoir, made in March 1885, are strongly marked by his latest triumphs, fusing Grant and the Civil War with the characters of *Huckleberry Finn*:

> Put Huck & Tom & Jim through my Mo. campaign & give a chapter to the Century.
> Union officer accosts Tom & says his name is US Grant.[87]

85. 18 Mar 1885 to Johnson, CtHMTH.
86. 16 Mar 1885 to Charles L. Webster, NPV, in *MTLP*, 184; see also the undated letter to Webster: "We want the Century's war book—keep on the best of terms with those folks" (NPV; probably written in 1885, misdated "August 1884?" in *MTLP*, 177–78); and "Grant's Memoirs," *AutoMT1*, 92.
87. *N&J3*, 105, entry probably made shortly before 20 March 1885.

On 26 May, Clemens visited Grant in New York and discussed his "Mo. campaign" with the general himself. His notebook entry of the same date shows the imaginative process hard at work: "I did not know that this was the future General Grant, or I would have turned & attacked him. I supposed it was just some ordinary Colonel, of no particular consequence, & so I let him go. It was probably a great mistake."[88] Around the same time, Clemens received from the *Century* editors some typed copies of General Nathaniel Lyon's June 1861 reports from the field, presumably intended to jog his historical memory.[89] But he did no serious work on the war paper until his family's removal to their summer home at Quarry Farm, near Elmira, New York, where they arrived on 19 June. An undated notebook entry provides a latest possible date for the first draft: "General said he read my article first & all the family afterward."[90] If this is true, a draft existed before 23 July, the date of Grant's death. An incomplete draft of some kind was in the hands of the *Century* editors before 30 July, when Buel referred to "the copy of your article left with us" and to "the remainder of the article,

88. *N&J3*, 152, entry dated 26 May 1885. It is often said that Clemens originally called his article "My Campaign against Grant," but this title seems to be Robert Underwood Johnson's suggestion (Johnson to SLC, 10 Aug 1885, CU-MARK; Mattson 1968a, 785).

89. *Century Magazine* to SLC, 22 May 1885, CU-MARK. The material sent to Clemens was copied from volume 3 of *The War of the Rebellion*, published in 1881 by the War Records Office (*OR*, 3:11–14). He annotated the envelope "Battles in Missouri in June '61," but no part of the information found its way into "The Private History."

90. *N&J3*, 152.

The Century Magazine, issue of December 1885. Mark Twain Papers.

as shaped in your head."[91] In late July, Clemens was playing for time: "I'm trying to get to work on that war paper again....But don't you wait for me—just jam in the other Generals and leave me to meander along in a kind of gravel-train fashion—which is my way."[92] His way was about to run up against the *Century*'s way, jovial and peremptory. "Work in all the maps you can, and all your Hardee," wrote Johnson, referring to a standard manual of infantry tactics.[93] Maps were a prominent feature of the *Century* series, and Clemens prepared three, two of which were reproduced in the final article. The editors' requirements were quite specific:

> For the purpose we are aiming at, ordinary "generals" will not do; we want a Missouri guerrilla of the most violent and humorous type, and we are perfectly willing to have you arrive on the gravel train you mention. Only do kindly "scratch gravel" in our interest and, if you will permit the suggestion, in *your* interest....We wish to have something about the War of universal interest, yet which will not be *too* military in its character. Pardon the implied insult to your professional skill.[94]

The *Century* wanted comedy, of the braggart-soldier variety: "Don't fail to bring out clearly that you were the only Confederate

91. Buel to SLC, 30 July 1885, CU-MARK. The editors read the draft version, for after completing a revision Clemens asked them to read the article "anew" (15 and 17 Aug 1885 to Johnson, CtHMTH).
92. 28 July 1885 to Johnson, published in Cyril Clemens 1945.
93. Johnson to SLC, 16 July 1885, CU-MARK.
94. Buel to SLC, 30 July 1885, CU-MARK.

that Grant really feared."[95] They offered to commission illustrations from Edward W. Kemble (1861–1933), whose pictures for *Huckleberry Finn* had decorated the *Century* extracts and the book publication.[96] Kemble was engaged, and his pictures would reinforce the text's vein of rustic farce.

The first draft would be subjected to two major revisions. Their chronology can be traced, but their content is unknown; due to the loss of manuscript material and the absence of detailed comment, we have only glimpses of the earlier versions. In Elmira on 10 August, Clemens began a revision, which he was able to report completed five days later:

> ...I have been grinding away at my war article, & have only finished it this moment. It may not be good enough yet, but it is better than it was before, anyway. It makes ostensibly 99 MS pages, but really only 80—that is to say, about 8 pages of the magazine. Mrs. Clemens will edit it to-night; I will re-edit it to-morrow, & then send it. I have made so many little alterations that I must ask you or Mr. Buell to read the *whole* of it anew, page by page. Then tell me what to strike out; also what to add, if anything occurs to you. If the passage about the old man reading his Bible & praying were stricken out, that would shorten the article noticeably; probably you or Mrs. Clemens will do that. There is a restraint about writing for the Century, somehow. It is not intemperate language to say it is the best magazine that was ever printed; & so, what would read quite fairly elsewhere, loses force & grace in the company of so much derned good writing.

95. Johnson to SLC, 10 Aug 1885, CU-MARK.
96. Buel to SLC, 30 July 1885, CU-MARK.

The "passage about the old man reading his Bible & praying," whatever it may have been, suffered as expected; but the changes did not stop there. Having written this letter, Clemens learned that his wife (Olivia Langdon Clemens, 1845–1904) was calling for a reformation far more sweeping than he had forecast. He explained in a postscript:

> P.S.—Monday, 17th, I've opened this to say the fat's all in the fire, for the present. Mrs. Clemens has convinced me that the article in its present shape has no sufficient raison d'etre. So I have begun it again, bran' new, today. I have hopes—but wait. It's a pretty thin subject, but I've started it on a modester plan this time.[97]

Since their marriage Olivia had, at her husband's invitation, served him as reader, critic, and censor, but the occasions on which she effected a complete tear-down were few indeed.

The revision process described here would leave Clemens with a certain amount of discarded manuscript, and in three surviving leaves that were used by him as gifts or souvenirs we glimpse an earlier state, or states, of the text. One leaf was given by Clemens to English clergyman George Bainton in October 1888. Bainton had written to dozens of the "leading authors of the day," representing himself as preparing a lecture on the compositional habits of literary people; he then created a minor stir by making unauthorized publication of the replies. Clemens's reply to Bainton (well known as the source of his saying about "the difference between the lightning-bug and the lightning")

97. 15 and 17 Aug 1885 to Johnson, CtHMTH.

Robert Underwood Johnson in his office at the *Century Magazine*, 1902. Photograph by Albert Bigelow Paine. Mark Twain Papers.

presumably had as enclosure the leaf numbered "94½," which contains a version of the text of 109.7–13.[98] Clemens inscribed it with his double signature and added a personal note to Bainton. Two more manuscript leaves, inscribed in the same way, were sent to an unknown recipient, who docketed both in purple ink: "Recd 9/7–1886."[99] One of these, numbered "77," bears the text of a fragmentary paragraph, asserting that Clemens's one battle was

98. Bainton to SLC, 6 Oct 1888, CU-MARK; 15 Oct 1888 to Bainton, CtHMTH; Bainton 1890. The MS leaf (MoSW) is reproduced on p. 59.

99. These manuscript leaves were formerly in the collection of John L. Feldman. Their current location is unknown.

much the bloodiest that was fought during the whole rebellion; therefore I have long felt that for this reason it was entitled to a place in the history of that conflict, & that no history of that conflict could justly be considered complete without some account of it. Indeed, with but one exception, it was the bloodiest battle that was ever fought, in any age or in any country.

This has no parallel in the published text, although the idea would survive to furnish the theme of Mark Twain's 8 April 1887 speech to Union veterans in Baltimore.[100] The other leaf, unnumbered, is Mark Twain's hand-drawn map showing the Rangers' route from Mason's/Matson's farm, through the "pasture," to "Camp Devastation."[101] The map's very point—that it is devoid of historical importance and strategic information—may have precipitated its exclusion from the published article.

The finished, twice-revised manuscript was dispatched to the *Century* offices, perhaps shortly before this 8 September 1885 letter to Johnson:

Mrs. Clemens has confessed, under cross-examination, that she does not like that article *yet.* Well, I've done all I could; it would be useless to try further. How would it answer to put it into the book, & leave it out of the magazine? In that case I will sell it to you for two dollars; & if you crowd me I will take less. I think its defects might be lost in the smoke & thunder of the big guns all around it in the book; but in the narrower & peacefuller field of the

100. SLC 1887.
101. Photocopy in CU-MARK.

magazine I think myself it will look like mighty poor weak stuff.[102]

On 11 September, Buel replied that the manuscript was already in the hands of the printers. He reassured the author: "Begging Mrs Clemens's pardon, it is a great advance on the first draft and in the opinion of *one* expert taster will be a great success with warriors as well as with the Peace Congress, and all Quakers."[103] The submission was late, and publication, which had been slated for the November issue, was delayed by one month.[104] It is not known what Clemens was paid. On 29 September Johnson wrote: "Did you overlook my inquiry in regard to the compensation for 'The Campaign That Failed,' or does your modesty forbid a reply?"; no reply from Clemens survives. In late August he had written in his notebook: "Century, $33.50 per page," at which rate the article would have brought him about four hundred dollars.[105] "The Private History" was published in the *Century Magazine* of 1 December 1885—the same day as the publication, by Webster and Company, of the first volume of Grant's *Personal Memoirs*, and also the day after Mark Twain's fiftieth birthday.

102. 8 Sept 1885 to Johnson, CU-MARK.

103. Buel to SLC, 11 Sept 1885, CU-MARK.

104. November publication is specified in Buel to SLC, 30 July 1885, CU-MARK, and in SLC to Redpath, 12 Sept 1885, transcript in CU-MARK.

105. Johnson to SLC, 29 Sept 1885, CU-MARK; *N&J3*, 179. "$33.50 per page" was Clemens's settled idea of the rate he commanded at the *Century Magazine* (*N&J2*, 437; *N&J3*, 10, 68, 179, 227).

Manuscript leaf of an early version of "The Private History," with Clemens's added note to George Bainton. George N. Meissner Collection, Washington University Libraries, Department of Special Collections.

4. "The fierce light that has beat upon your chronicle"

In the case of Mark Twain's paper, the *Century* editors' intention to "soften controversy" would be defeated. While it is true that more newspapers excerpted the text for their readers' enjoyment than denounced it, his "modest" contribution had opened a field for response—which, when it came, was a wave of indignation and condemnation unusual in the history of his public reception. On 13 December 1885 several newspapers published a story said to emanate from certain "Union veterans" offended by Clemens's revelation of his past, "heretofore not generally known," as a "rebel guerilla." This report inaugurated an enduring criticism of the story: that Mark Twain excuses his irresponsibility and buffoonery as the behavior natural to a man of "twenty-four" (in June 1861 he was in fact twenty-five). So said the Washington *Post*:

> The account by the humorist of his campaign, just published in the *Century*, seeks to turn the thing into ridicule, and to make it out a mere holiday escapade of boys, with no seriousness of intention or consequence on the part of the fifteen members of the company. But Twain was then twenty-four years old, and the band of which he was lieutenant did some quite wicked marauding. The killing of the non-combatant stranger, narrated in his article incidentally, is said by his enemies to have been susceptible of a different construction.[106]

106. "Mark Twain's 'War Paper,'" Washington *Post*, 13 Dec 1885, 4; the same information appeared, on the same date, in the following: "Mark

The Boston *Record* editorialized that for Mark Twain to blame his recruits' foolishness on their youth was a slander on young veterans: "A multitude of elect youths showed the maturity of courage at an age when Mark Twain says there is, as a rule, not much attention paid to details."[107] At least one private citizen raised the same point. From a railway car near Erie, Pennsylvania, on 23 December 1885, a Mr. C. A. Martin wrote:

Dear Sir,

I have just read your paper in the December "Century"—I think in such a matter as this I represent the average reader, & so my opinion should have some value to you. I am very sorry you published such a story—It seems to me to be a pity that I have seen the self displayed nakedness of a man whom I have enjoyed & admired to some extent—If you have a boy I hope he has not read this shameful story of cowardice & folly—*24* years old! & man enough to have been a river pilot—I was a Captain at *21*, after having served from the age of 19—Custer was a Major Genl.

Twain as a Guerilla," Boston *Herald*, 16; "Willy Wally Astor," Chicago *Tribune*, 25; and "Astor and Twain," Milwaukee *Sentinel*, 12. These articles traced the anti-Twain rumors and grumbles to certain "Union veterans" who were canvassing for a new Civil War book, and who resented the ex-rebel Mark Twain for profiting from Grant's memoirs. The reference is probably to the Historical Publishing Company of Philadelphia, which in the summer of 1885 issued a circular attempting to damage the sale of Grant's book. The circular listed eleven reasons why the book would be unattractive to canvassers and agents and would prove unremunerative (*N&J3*, 183; circular in Scrapbook 22, 88, CU-MARK; enclosure with Webster to SLC, 20 Aug 1885, CU-MARK).

107. "In his contribution in The Century…," Milwaukee *Sentinel*, 8 Dec 1885, 4, reprinting the Boston *Record* of unknown date.

at 23, & the gallants captain & Colonels & Brigadiers in both armies, under 23, could be named by hundreds—24 was *pretty old,* in those days—And you, a man of 24, hiding away in terror, from rumors proved false a hundred times, fired from the inside of a log hut, upon an unarmed & uniformed man—

The story is revolting & disgusting—and the shamelessness of its voluntary recital, is one of the strangest facts in literature—

Ys &c

C. A. Martin.

I think the story is a fancy sketch—no such poltroons & fools existed any where—and your own lack of sensibility has let you put yourself into it, at the age of

24!

On the envelope Clemens wrote: "anonymous *ass.*"[108] But he saved the letter.

In his regular column for the Chicago *News,* the poet and journalist Eugene Field (1850–95), best known today as the author of "Little Boy Blue" and "Wynken, Blynken, and Nod," condemned both matter and manner:

> Mark Twain has contributed to the December Century an article upon a war experience of his that is anything but entertaining, and is certainly far from being in the slightest degree humorous. He tells in a very cold-blooded way of the formation during the

108. CU-MARK.

war of a company of young southern ruffians. There were only fifteen members, including Twain, and from the latter's own statement we should judge that they were on a par with the average hoodlum of to-day. The company does not seem to have been organized in the interests of the confederacy, and it lacked even the semi-respectable dignity of the guerrillas, employing its time in lawlessness which the excited state of the country permitted. The chief point of the article is the relation of the murder by this gang of an inoffensive stranger who happened to ride into that neighborhood. It is spoken of by Twain as quite a commonplace incident—as likely enough it was to such lawless banditti—but it cannot even at this late day help raising a feeling of abhorrence and disgust in the reader. It is an experience of which Twain should be too ashamed to speak, even if it *had* occurred in his youth, as he says it did, though it did not, for he was 24 years old at the time. It certainly shows him in very black colors.[109]

As the fire of indignation moved westward, the flames were fanned by John I. Ginn (1835–1916), a roving newspaperman who had been acquainted with Clemens in Virginia City, Nevada, during the Civil War. Ginn, "a snorting Democrat" who laid claim to Confederate service and who "started more newspapers than any other man in the profession of journalism,"[110] was

109. Field 1885. Clemens and Field seem to have met just once, in Chicago in April 1893. After Field's death, Clemens wrote of him: "I knew Eugene Field a little. He gave me a pleasant hour when I was on my back in the doctor's hands, once. It was a great loss to literature & good-fellowship when he got his freedom" (10 Oct 1898 to Senour, photocopy in CU-MARK).

110. "Bean & Ginn…," Rocklin (Calif.) *Placer Herald,* 6 Apr 1872, 2; "John I. Ginn…," Carson City *Appeal,* 1 Feb 1884, 3; "Nevada State

currently the owner and editor of the Nogales (Arizona Territory) *Weekly Frontier*, which ran this story in January 1886:

Some of the Eastern literary papers seem to have just discovered that Mark Twain (Samuel L. Clemens) was a rebel bushwhacker in the early part of the late war. The fact was published in Virginia, Nevada, in 1864, during the hottest period of the war. And worse—the rival journal that published the fact went further, and intimated in language not to be mistaken that Mark had violated his parole, and was then a fit subject for a target for a detail of Union soldiers.

Lieutenant Clemens, having been a pilot on the Mississippi river, and therefore knowing the channel and being familiar with the points where steamboats would have to hug the shore, was detailed for the special duty of firing into the Federal transports plying that stream—and he performed the duty effectively. He was captured and paroled. While under parole, the account stated, he went ahead firing into Union boats. He was captured a second time, but by a different command—none of whom knew he was under parole, or he would have been shot on the spot. He was sent to St. Louis and imprisoned in a tobacco warehouse on Wash avenue. He got to thinking the matter over—the probability of being sent to Grant's army, by which he was first captured, to be exchanged, and by which, if recognized, he would certainly be shot for a violation of his parole—and he skipped across the plains to the Territory of Nevada, of which his brother, Orion Clemens, was then Secretary by appointment from President Lincoln. Fear-

Journal," Reno *Nevada State Journal*, 23 Nov 1870, 6; "Personals," Reno *Gazette-Journal*, 1 Oct 1885, 3; El Paso *Herald*: "Capt. John Ginn Dies; Aged 81," 21 Nov 1916, 10; "Funeral of Capt. Ginn," 23 Nov 1916, 8; McKinnon 2004, 324–37.

ing the influence of his brother would not be sufficient to save him if he should be recognized by passing officers or soldiers of the Union army, he did not remain long in Carson City, but pushed on to the out-of-the-way mining camp of Aurora, where he remained until he fancied the storm had blown over.

While in Aurora he wrote a series of letters to the *Virginia Enterprise*, and subsequently accepted a place on the editorial staff of that journal. His sharp pen put a man named Willis, city editor of the *Virginia Union*, to hunting up his record, and the publication of the foregoing facts was the result. For this, Mark Twain sent Willis a challenge to mortal combat. The challenge was sent by Mark's "game" little friend, Steve Gillis. Willis would not accept— he would not meet any one on the field of honor except a man of honor. This offended Gillis highly, and he challenged Willis. Willis would not accept, because he had no cause of quarrel with Gillis, but his "best man" then came in and challenged Mark Twain, who declined on the same ground given by Willis for not meeting Gillis. The three challenges all passed the same day—within a few hours, in fact—and as duelling had just been made popular by the Dog Valley meeting of Tom Fitch, "the silver-tongued" orator, and Joseph T. Goodman, the poetical editor-in-chief of the *Enterprise*, it looked for a time as though Six-Mile Cañon was to be deluged with blood. But the matter was dropped, and Mark Twain was never called upon by a drumhead court-martial to stand up and take the regulation dose of leaden pills.[111]

"This isn't as funny as the story that Mark tells," commented the St. Louis *Globe-Democrat*, "but there is reason to believe that for

111. "Mark Twain. What John I. Ginn Knows about His War Record," San Francisco *Alta California*, 1 Feb 1886, 7, reprinting the Nogales (Arizona Territory) *Frontier* of unknown date.

historical purposes it is more reliable."[112] Actually, where Ginn's story can be checked—that is, in the final paragraph—it seems to be a garbled account of Clemens's dueling challenge to James Laird, of the Virginia *Union,* in May 1864. At that time Ginn was a printer for the Virginia City *Old Piute,* and well placed to hear about Clemens's challenge; everyone involved was a local printer or journalist.[113] The record shows that a *Union* printer named Wilmington (not an "editor" named "Willis") published a letter calling the editor of the *Enterprise* a "*liar, a poltroon, and a puppy*" for slandering the printers of the *Union.* Clemens replied that he had written the offending editorial and the insult was meant for him. He challenged Laird, the *Union*'s owner, and refused to duel when Wilmington put himself forward; then Wilmington refused to duel with Clemens's second, Steve Gillis, when *he* put himself forward. It is clearly this affair that Ginn recalls, but no material known to us validates Ginn's claim that the Civil War record he attributes to Clemens was published in the Virginia *Union.*[114] It must be noted that the surviving

112. "It appears that Mark Twain's recent account…," St. Louis *Globe-Democrat,* 17 Feb 1886, 6.

113. Collins 1864–65, 68 (Clemens), 88 (Gillis), 88 (Ginn), 213 (Wilmington), 108 (Laird); Doten 1973, 3:2252; "Gillis's Whiskey Spring," Carson *Appeal,* 29 Aug 1880, 3.

114. Most of the published and unpublished correspondence is reprinted in *MTEnt,* 185–205; for Wilmington's first letter in the Virginia *Union,* see Mack 1947, 316. Steve Gillis's account of the (non-)duel is in *MTB,* 1:250–51. Ginn's version of events was repeated in an 1892 hack biography of Mark Twain, and passed in 1910 into many newspaper obituaries (Will M. Clemens 1892, 39–40; " 'Mark Twain' Dies of Broken Heart as Shadows Fall," Philadelphia *Inquirer,* 22 Apr 1910, 13; "Death

files of that paper are incomplete, and it remains possible that Wilmington, after Clemens refused to fight him, published an item now lost, reflecting on Clemens's rebel past. But the rebel past Ginn claims for Clemens is outlandish: military and civilian records show no trace of this supposed history of capture, parole, recapture, imprisonment, and escape, and his supposed encounter with "Grant's army" is quite incompatible with his joy at discovering, in 1885, that he had ever been anywhere near Grant's army.[115]

Absalom Grimes's 1886 account of the campaign, which is presented as a direct response to "The Private History," has already been discussed. As a participant in the events he describes, Grimes is in a totally different class from the rumor-mongers Bixby and Ginn. He is certainly the only one of all these biographers and autobiographers to give personal references. In his 1876 "interview" he said Mark Twain himself would "vouch for the truth of this story, any time"; ten years later he was not so sure of that, and listed Nuck Matson and Asa Glascock as "'well-to-do' farmers, [who] can vouch for the little sketch I have given you of Mark Twain's war record."[116] He provides their current contact information.

Before continuing with the reception of "The Private History," we may pause to discredit an apocryphal tale circulated in 1910 by the lawyer and orator Tom Fitch (1838–1923), who had

of Mark Twain," [Bombay] *Times of India*, 23 Apr 1910, 9; "Life Story of Mark Twain," Dallas *News*, 24 Apr 1910, 28; etc.).

115. See p. 37.

116. Grimes 1876.

known Clemens in Virginia City in 1863–64. Fitch's tale sets Clemens in a chaotic Missouri run by a secessionist governor and a Unionist lieutenant governor. Their contradictory orders finally extract from Clemens this supposed letter of resignation:

> "Sir: I respectfully resign my membership of and my commission as captain of Co. B. Hannibal Home Guard. I am perfectly willing to fight for either the United States or the Confederacy, but this damned uncertainty as to which side I am on is killing me with anxiety. With assurances of my high consideration, I am respectfully yours, etc."
>
> Mark said: "I was troubled in my conscience a little, for I had enlisted, and was not clear as to my lawful right to disenlist. But I remembered that one of the conditions of joining was that the members of the guard should not be required to leave their home towns except in case of invasion of the State by an enemy. The Confederate forces had invaded Southwest Missouri. I saw at once that in accordance with the terms of enlistment I was required to leave the State, and I left at once by the overland route to Nevada, of which Territory my brother, Orion Clemens, had been appointed Secretary."[117]

---

117. Fitch 1910; 11 Nov 1864 to OC, *L1*, 318–19 n. 4. Fitch's reticence about the source of his quotation has had consequences, for it is popular with biographers, not all of whom note its uncertain status. Irving Coryell treats it as early newspaper writing by Clemens for the Virginia City *Territorial Enterprise*, while Arthur G. Pettit treats it as a personal letter from Clemens to Fitch in "1864." Gary Scharnhorst treats the resignation as a letter to "John Ralls," and the ensuing comment as a personal communication to Fitch "sixty years later" (Coryell 1937, 289–90; Pettit 1974, 183 and 212 n. 1; Scharnhorst 2018, 135).

Even if we grant the idea of Clemens formally resigning, as opposed to simply deserting, and leaving aside the absurd historical setting (Missouri's lieutenant governor, Thomas C. Reynolds, was no Unionist) and the erroneous details ("commission," "captain," "Home Guard"), Fitch cannot in any case have seen such a letter. If his report has any basis, it is in Clemens's conversation, or else in some Mark Twain publication otherwise unknown; worthless as history, it may yet record one of Clemens's own characteristically distorted autobiographical narratives.

The Century Company had planned all along to republish the completed war series, with added material, as a multi-volume book. In the spring of 1887 "The Private History" was still expected to take its place in the Century "war book," yet the editors' correspondence with Clemens betrays anxiety over the article's troubled reception. Robert Underwood Johnson wrote to Clemens on 10 February 1887, enclosing book proofs: "You will see from this inclosure that we are squinting toward the War Book. Will you kindly look over the proofs once more, in the fierce light that has beat upon your chronicle?" Here Clemens saw an opportunity to suppress the "cruelty" he had inflicted upon John RoBards in satirizing him as "d'Un Lap." Johnson was accommodating, inviting him to attack the proofs: "Cut out what you wish to omit....If you cut out anything else let it be of things that are *least intimately* (isn't that delicately put?) associated *with the actual conflict of arms*. But we dont care to lose any of it. If any man says it isn't part of the serious history of the War, we'll tell him we're trying to change the serious character of war-history."[118]

We know Clemens carried out his RoBards suppression on the proofs, for on 19 April 1887 he wrote to a Hannibal acquaintance: "Please give my warmest regards to the Garths, & say I was ashamed of putting that 'd'Un Lap' cruelty into that 'Century' article, & so I have stricken it out & it will not appear in the Century's War book. I think John Robards deserved a lashing, but it should have come from an enemy, not a friend."[119] The proofs are not extant, and exactly what revisions he made must remain a mystery; for as the parts making up the first volume of *Battles and Leaders of the Civil War* were published, starting in June 1887, it was observable that "The Private History" had been replaced with a paper by Thomas L. Snead.[120] Snead (1828–90) had recently published a first-hand account of the war in Missouri, drawing on his experiences as an aide to Claiborne Jackson and a staff officer to Sterling Price. Whereas the *Century* editors had steered Clemens toward a production "not…*too* military in its character," they now turned to Snead for the "*actual conflict of arms.*" While no correspondence bearing

118. Johnson to SLC, 10 Feb 1887 and 27 Mar 1887, both in CU-MARK.

119. 19 Apr 1887 to John Davis, ViU. For John L. RoBards, see pp. 34–35 and pp. 117–18, note on 81.11–82.26.

120. The Century Company book is usually encountered bound in four volumes, but it was first published in thirty-two separate parts between June 1887 and June 1889. Snead's paper, "The First Year of the War in Missouri," was in volume 1, part 3, published in August 1887 ("Literary Notes," *Independent* 39 [23 June 1887]: 10; "The third number…," Hartford *Courant*, 1 Aug 1887, 4; "Battles and Leaders of the Civil War," *Critic* 11 [8 June 1889]: 279–80).

upon the suppression and replacement of "The Private History" has been found, it looks as though the editors had succumbed to the criticism, mentioned in Johnson's letter, that Mark Twain's paper was not "part of the serious history of the war." As finally issued, Snead's contribution to *Battles and Leaders* retained but a single trace of its precursor: on its first page, Edward Kemble's initial capital (p. 79) was repurposed as an illustration captioned "A Very Raw Recruit."[121]

The writing and publication of "The Private History" did nothing to stabilize Clemens's subsequent approach to the events of the summer of 1861. Like all his experiences, they remained permanently available, to be worked and reworked as occasion offered. For his speech to Union veterans in Baltimore on 8 April 1887, he cannibalized a discarded portion of the "Private History" manuscript. He had been asked, he said, to "clear up a matter which…had long been a subject of dispute and bad blood in war circles in this country—to wit, the true dimensions of my military service in the civil war, and the effect which they had upon the general result."[122] Having thus alluded to the troubled reception of his war paper, Clemens plowed ahead with the self-aggrandizing claim he had made in an early version of "The Private History": his one battle, he said, was "the bloodiest battle ever fought in human history," inasmuch as the opposing force (of one man) had been "utterly exterminated." Such terrible destructive power would have made the war "too

121. Snead 1886; Johnson and Buel 1887–89, 1:262.
122. SLC 1887.

one-sided," so he withdrew "to give the Union cause a chance."

About four years later, in a draft letter to an unknown recipient, Clemens argued the position that "the most valuable capital, or culture, or education usable in the building of novels is personal experience." He inventoried his stock of experiences, declaring himself "familiar" with war:

> I was a *soldier* two weeks, once, in the beginning of the war, & was hunted like a rat the whole time. Familiar? My splendid Kipling himself hasn't a more burnt-in, hard-baked & unforgetable familiarity with that death-on-the-pale-horse-with-hell-following-after which is a raw soldier's first fortnight in the field—& which, without any doubt, is the most tremendous fortnight & the vividest he is ever going to see.[123]

We could well wish for such a sketch from Mark Twain, though clearly it, too, would have little claim to be definitive.

Perhaps the truth is that Clemens's attitude toward the war was less informed by his brief military experience than by the long era that followed. The postwar period demanded of a public figure that he account for his deeds and his loyalties, answer or dodge the big questions, and promote reconciliation while simultaneously asserting the integrity of both factions. Such demands called for flexibility, a quality much in evidence in Clemens's remarks at a Carnegie Hall event honoring Abraham Lincoln on 11 February 1901. This forms a rare exception to the

123. "After February 1891" (draft) to unidentified recipient, CU-MARK, reprinted in *MTB*, 2:915–16.

Lincoln-shaped hole in Mark Twain's writing—an omission that might be understood as the result of guilt over his conduct in the time of crisis, were it not obvious that neither his former loyalties nor any shame about changing them prevented his fervent participation in the cult of Ulysses S. Grant. Having come at last to publicly celebrate Lincoln, Mark Twain attested his "reverence and love of that noble soul whom forty years ago we tried with all our hearts and all our strength to defeat and dispossess," and expressed satisfaction that the North had triumphed; yet into this vein of Union celebration there obtruded a compensatory validation of the South:

> Those were great days, splendid days. What an uprising it was! For the hearts of the whole nation, North and South, were in the war. We of the South were not ashamed, for like the men of the North we were fighting for what we believed with all our sincere souls to be our rights; on both sides we were fighting for our homes and hearthstones, and for the honor of the flags we loved; and when men fight for these things, and under these convictions, with nothing sordid to tarnish their cause, that cause is holy, the blood spilt in it is sacred, the life that is laid down for it is consecrated. To-day we no longer regret the result; to-day we are glad it came out as it did; but we are not ashamed that we did our endeavor; we did our bravest and best, against desperate odds, for the cause which was precious to us and which our consciences approved: and we are proud—and you are proud—the kindred blood in your veins answers when I say it—you are proud of the record we made in those mighty collisions in the field.[124]

124. The speech is quoted here from its earliest full publication, "by permission of Mr. Clemens," in SLC 1901, which differs significantly from

Today we struggle to explain this uncharacteristic burst of "Lost Cause" rhetoric, wondering, among other things, how Mark Twain and his audience contrived to reconcile this paean to the "splendid days" of the Civil War with his own abrupt departure to hunt for gold and silver far from the field of battle. Yet it was Mark Twain's praise of Lincoln, not his rebel idyll, which pained one newspaper reader:

Mr. Mark Twain;
    Dear Sir:
   When I read your article in the *North American Review* I hoped to see you President of the United States in 1905. Think, then, with what revulsion of feeling I read what you had to say at the Lincoln Birthday hullabulloo! How *came* you to be so sinfully reconstructed? My father used to own a large plantation, with slaves to match, and here I am on the top floor of a working women's boarding house, fairly fighting for my life. In the latter respect I am but one of thousands of Southern women. Unlike the Rev. Thomas Dixon, whose father never owned any slaves (to speak of) I do not "rejoice that, owing to the Emancipation Act, my childhood was passed in poverty." When you next open your *Mother Goose* and read about Taffy the Welshman, think of Abe Lincoln.
                    Your ex-admirer,
                    Clara Marshall[125]

newspaper reports and from the texts published posthumously by Harper and Brothers ("Blue and Gray Pay Tribute to Lincoln," New York *Times*, 12 Feb 1901, 1; SLC 1910, 295–97; *MTB*, 3:1123–24; SLC 1923, 228–31). Fatout 1976 (381–83) prints a conflation of the four last named sources.

125. Clara Marshall to SLC, 27 Feb 1901, CU-MARK. Marshall alludes to Mark Twain's article "To the Person Sitting in Darkness," published in the *North American Review* in February 1901; and to Southern-born, New

Clemens annotated the envelope: "Use in Corn-pone," referring to "Corn-Pone Opinions," an essay he wrote around this time. It expounds a view Clemens says he picked up in his youth from a black slave: "You tell me whar a man gits his corn-pone, en I'll tell you what his 'pinions is." Clara Marshall's letter is not used in the essay, but certainly it furnishes perfect material, so clearly does her aversion to Lincoln result from her own loss of property and status after Emancipation. Yet in his Lincoln Birthday speech Mark Twain is looking to his own corn-pone, and he knows it. "A man's self-approval, in the large concerns of life, has its source in the approval of the people about him, and not in a searching personal examination of the matter....Broadly speaking, there are none but corn-pone opinions."[126]

Less well known than Mark Twain's sayings are the things he refused to say. In 1907 he received four letters, one of them being from the governor of Missouri, inviting him to lecture for the benefit of the St. Louis chapter of the United Daughters of the Confederacy, their goal being the construction of a monument to the Confederate dead in the city's Forest Park. Through his secretary, he declined.[127] The thirty-two-foot monument would be built and dedicated in 1914, four years after Clemens's death.

York–based preacher and writer Thomas Dixon, Jr. (1864–1946), best known as the author of *The Clansman* (1905).

126. *WIM*, 92–97 and 595–96.

127. United Confederate Veterans to SLC, 20 Mar 1907; James B. Gantt and Leroy B. Valliant to SLC, 29 March 1907; Joseph Folle to SLC, 3 Apr 1907; Mrs. W. G. Moore to SLC, 4 Apr 1907 (all CU-MARK). Clemens's secretary, Isabel V. Lyon, noted on three of the letters that she answered them on 16 April. On the monument, see Burkhardt 2011.

It stood until 2017, when, amid a national controversy over Confederate monuments, the St. Louis city council ordered it to be removed. This was done, over the objections of those who thought nothing needed to change.[128] At the outbreak of the Civil War, Clemens had held such a belief; fleeing the battle, he lived and learned to know better.

Benjamin Griffin
Berkeley, 2018

128. "In Popular Park, a Point of Contention," New York *Times*, 27 May 2017, A10; "Disputed Monument Almost Gone," St. Louis *Post-Dispatch*, 29 June 2017, A7.

THE PRIVATE HISTORY OF A CAMPAIGN THAT FAILED

Y ou have heard from a great many people who did something in the war; is it not fair and right that you listen a little moment to one who started out to do something in it, but didn't? Thousands entered the war, got just a taste of it, and then stepped out again, permanently. These, by their very numbers, are respectable, and are therefore entitled to a sort of voice,—not a loud one, but a modest one; not a boastful one, but an apologetic one. They ought not to be allowed much space among better people— people who did something—I grant that; but they ought at least to be allowed to state why they didn't do anything, and also to explain the process by which they didn't do anything. Surely this kind of light must have a sort of value.

Out West there was a good deal of confusion in men's minds during the first months of the great trouble—a good deal of unsettledness, of leaning first this way, then that, then the other way. It was hard for us to get our bearings. I call to mind an instance of this. I was piloting on the Mississippi when the news came that South Carolina had gone out of the Union on the

20th of December, 1860. My pilot-mate was a New Yorker. He was strong for the Union; so was I. But he would not listen to me with any patience; my loyalty was smirched, to his eye, because my father had owned slaves. I said, in palliation of this dark fact, that I had heard my father say, some years before he died, that slavery was a great wrong, and that he would free the solitary negro he then owned if he could think it right to give away the property of the family when he was so straitened in means. My mate retorted that a mere impulse was nothing—anybody could pretend to a good impulse; and went on decrying my Unionism and libeling my ancestry. A month later the secession atmosphere had considerably thickened on the Lower Mississippi, and I became a rebel; so did he. We were together in New Orleans, the 26th of January, when Louisiana went out of the Union. He did his full share of the rebel shouting, but was bitterly opposed to letting me do mine. He said that I came of bad stock—of a father who had been willing to set slaves free. In the following summer he was piloting a Federal gun-boat and shouting for the Union again, and I was in the Confederate army. I held his note for some borrowed money. He was one of the most upright men I ever knew; but he repudiated that note without hesitation, because I was a rebel, and the son of a man who owned slaves.

In that summer—of 1861—the first wash of the wave of war broke upon the shores of Missouri. Our State was invaded by the Union forces. They took possession of St. Louis, Jefferson Barracks, and some other points. The Governor, Claib Jackson, issued his proclamation calling out fifty thousand militia to repel the invader.

The Seat of War.

I was visiting in the small town where my boyhood had been spent—Hannibal, Marion County. Several of us got together in a secret place by night and formed ourselves into a military company. One Tom Lyman, a young fellow of a good deal of spirit but of no military experience, was made captain; I was made second lieutenant. We had no first lieutenant; I do not know why; it was long ago. There were fifteen of us. By the advice of an innocent connected with the organization, we called ourselves the Marion Rangers. I do not remember that any one found fault with the name. I did not; I thought it sounded quite well. The young fellow who proposed this title was perhaps a fair sample of the kind of stuff we were made of. He was young, ignorant, good-natured, well-meaning, trivial, full of romance, and given to reading chivalric novels and singing forlorn love-ditties. He had some pathetic little nickel-plated aristocratic instincts, and detested his name, which was Dunlap; detested it, partly because it was nearly as common in that region as Smith, but mainly because it had a plebeian sound to his ear. So he tried to ennoble it by writing it in this way: *d'Unlap*. That contented his eye, but left his ear unsatisfied, for people gave the new name the same old pronunciation—emphasis on the front end of it. He then did the bravest thing that can be imagined,—a thing to make one shiver when one remembers how the world is given to resenting shams and affectations; he began to write his name so: *d'Un Lap*. And he waited patiently through the long storm of mud that was flung at this work of art, and he had his reward at last; for he lived to see that name accepted, and the emphasis put where he wanted it, by people who had known him all his life, and to whom the tribe of Dunlaps had been as familiar as the rain and the sunshine for forty years. So sure of victory at last is the courage that can wait. He said he had found, by consulting some ancient French chronicles, that the name was rightly and originally written d'Un Lap; and said that if it were translated into English it would mean Peterson: *Lap*, Latin or Greek, he said, for stone or rock, same as the French *pierre*, that is to say, Peter; *d'*, of or from; *un*, a or one; hence, d'Un Lap, of or from a stone or a Peter; that is to say, one who is the son of a stone, the son of a Peter—Peterson. Our militia company were not learned, and the explanation confused them; so they called him Peterson Dunlap. He proved useful to us in his way; he named our camps for us, and he generally struck a name that was "no slouch," as the boys said.

PETERSON D'UN LAP.

That is one sample of us. Another was Ed Stevens, son of the town jeweler,—trim-built, handsome, graceful, neat as a cat; bright, educated, but given over entirely to fun. There was nothing serious in life to him. As far as he was concerned, this military expedition of ours was simply a holiday. I should say that about half of us looked upon it in the same way; not consciously, perhaps, but unconsciously. We did not think; we were not capable of it. As for myself, I was full of unreasoning joy to be done with turning out of bed at midnight and four in the morning, for a while; grateful to have a change, new scenes, new occupations, a new interest. In my thoughts that was as far as I went; I did not go into the details; as a rule one doesn't at twenty-four.

Another sample was Smith, the blacksmith's apprentice. This vast donkey had some pluck, of a slow and sluggish nature, but a soft heart; at one time he would knock a horse down for some impropriety, and at another he would get homesick and cry. However, he had one ultimate credit to his account which some of us hadn't: he stuck to the war, and was killed in battle at last.

Jo Bowers, another sample, was a huge, good-natured, flax-headed lubber; lazy, sentimental, full of harmless brag, a grumbler by nature; an experienced, industrious, ambitious, and often quite picturesque liar, and yet not a successful one, for he had had no intelligent training, but was allowed to come up just any way. This life was serious enough to him, and seldom satisfactory. But he was a good fellow anyway, and the boys all liked him. He was made orderly sergeant; Stevens was made corporal.

These samples will answer—and they are quite fair ones. Well, this herd of cattle started for the war. What could you expect of them? They did as well as they knew how, but really what was justly to be expected of them? Nothing, I should say. That is what they did.

We waited for a dark night, for caution and secrecy were necessary; then, toward midnight, we stole in couples and from various directions to the Griffith place, beyond the town; from that point we set out together on foot. Hannibal lies at the extreme south-eastern corner of Marion County, on the Mississippi River; our objective point was the hamlet of New London, ten miles away, in Ralls County.

The first hour was all fun, all idle nonsense and laughter. But that could not be kept up. The steady trudging came to be like work; the play had somehow oozed out of it; the stillness of the woods and the somberness of the night began to throw a depressing influence over the spirits of the boys, and presently the talking died out and each person shut himself up in his own thoughts. During the last half of the second hour nobody said a word.

Now we approached a log farm-house where, according to report, there was a guard of five Union soldiers. Lyman called a halt; and there, in the deep gloom of the overhanging branches, he began to whisper a plan of assault upon that house, which made the gloom more depressing than it was before. It was a crucial moment; we realized, with a cold suddenness, that here was no jest—we were standing face to face with actual war. We were equal to the occasion. In our response there was no hesitation, no indecision: we said that if Lyman wanted to meddle with those soldiers, he could go ahead and do it; but if he waited for us to follow him, he would wait a long time.

Lyman urged, pleaded, tried to shame us, but it had no effect. Our course was plain, our minds were made up: we would flank the farm-house—go out around. And that is what we did.

We struck into the woods and entered upon a rough time, stumbling over roots, getting tangled in vines, and torn by briers. At last we reached an open place in a safe region, and sat down, blown and hot, to cool off and nurse our scratches and bruises. Lyman was annoyed, but the rest of us were cheerful; we had flanked the farm-house, we had made our first military movement, and it was a success; we had nothing to fret about, we were feeling just the other way. Horse-play and laughing began again; the expedition was become a holiday frolic once more.

Then we had two more hours of dull trudging and ultimate silence and depression; then, about dawn, we straggled into New London, soiled, heel-blistered, fagged with our little march, and all of us except Stevens in a sour and raspy humor and privately down on the war. We stacked our shabby old shot-guns in Colonel Ralls's barn, and then went in a body and breakfasted with that veteran of the Mexican war. Afterwards he took us to a distant meadow, and there in the shade of a tree we listened to an old-fashioned speech from him, full of gunpowder and glory, full of that adjective-piling, mixed metaphor, and windy declamation which was regarded as eloquence in that ancient time and that remote region; and then he swore us on the Bible to be faithful to the State of Missouri and drive all invaders from her soil, no matter whence they might come or under what flag they might march. This mixed us considerably, and we could not make out just what service we were embarked in; but Colonel Ralls, the practiced politician and phrase-juggler, was not similarly in doubt; he knew quite clearly that he had invested us in the cause of the Southern Confederacy. He closed the solemnities by belting around me the sword which his neighbor, Colonel Brown, had worn at Buena Vista and Molino del Rey; and he accompanied this act with another impressive blast.

THE SWORD OF BUENA VISTA AND MOLINO DEL REY.

Then we formed in line of battle and marched four miles to a shady and pleasant piece of woods on the border of the far-reaching expanses of a flowery prairie. It was an enchanting region for war—our kind of war.

We pierced the forest about half a mile, and took up a strong position, with some low, rocky, and wooded hills behind us, and a purling, limpid creek in front. Straightway half the command were in swimming, and the other half fishing. The ass with the French name gave this position a romantic title, but it was too long, so the boys shortened and simplified it to Camp Ralls.

We occupied an old maple-sugar camp, whose half-rotted troughs were still propped against the trees. A long corn-crib served for sleeping quarters for the battalion. On our left, half a mile away, was Mason's farm and house; and he was a friend to the cause.

Shortly after noon the farmers began to arrive from several directions, with mules and horses for our use, and these they lent us for as long as the war might last, which they judged would be about three months. The animals were of all sizes, all colors, and all breeds. They were mainly young and frisky, and nobody in the command could stay on them long at a time; for we were town boys, and ignorant of horsemanship. The creature that fell to my share was a very small mule, and yet so quick and active that it could throw me without difficulty; and it did this whenever I got on it. Then it would bray—stretching its neck out, laying its ears back, and spreading its jaws till you could see down to its works. It was a disagreeable animal, in every way. If I took it by the bridle and tried to lead it off the grounds, it would sit down and brace back, and no one could budge it. However, I was not entirely destitute of military resources, and I did presently manage to spoil this game; for I had seen many a steamboat aground in my time, and knew a trick or two which even a grounded mule would be obliged to respect. There was a well by the corn-crib; so I substituted thirty fathom of rope for the bridle, and fetched him home with the windlass.

I will anticipate here sufficiently to say that we did learn to ride, after some days' practice, but never well. We could not learn to like our animals; they were not choice ones, and most of them had annoying peculiarities of one kind or another. Stevens's horse would carry him, when he was not noticing, under the huge excrescences which form on the trunks of oak-trees, and wipe him out of the saddle; in this way Stevens got several bad hurts. Sergeant Bowers's horse was very large and tall, with slim, long legs, and looked like a railroad bridge. His size enabled him to reach all about, and as far as he wanted to, with his head; so he was always biting Bowers's legs. On the march, in the sun, Bowers slept a good deal; and as soon as the horse recognized that he was asleep he would reach around and bite him on the leg. His legs were black and blue with bites. This was the only thing that could ever make him swear, but this always did; whenever the horse bit him he always swore, and of course Stevens, who laughed at everything, laughed at this, and would even get into such convulsions over it as to lose his balance and fall off his horse; and then Bowers, already irritated by the pain of the horse-bite, would resent the laughter with hard language, and there would be a quarrel; so that horse made no end of trouble and bad blood in the command.

However, I will get back to where I was—our first afternoon in the sugar-camp. The sugar-troughs came very handy as horse-troughs, and we had plenty of corn to fill them with. I ordered

Sergeant Bowers to feed my mule; but he said that if I reckoned he went to war to be dry-nurse to a mule, it wouldn't take me very long to find out my mistake. I believed that this was insubordination, but I was full of uncertainties about everything military, and so I let the thing pass, and went and ordered Smith, the blacksmith's apprentice, to feed the mule; but he merely gave me a large, cold, sarcastic grin, such as an ostensibly seven-year-old horse gives you when you lift his lip and find he is fourteen, and turned his back on me. I then went to the captain, and asked if it was not right and proper and military for me to have an orderly. He said it was, but as there was only one orderly in the corps, it was but right that he himself should have Bowers on his staff. Bowers said he wouldn't serve on anybody's staff; and if anybody thought he could make him, let him try it. So, of course, the thing had to be dropped; there was no other way.

Next, nobody would cook; it was considered a degradation; so we had no dinner. We lazied the rest of the pleasant afternoon away, some dozing under the trees, some smoking cob-pipes and talking sweethearts and war, some playing games. By late suppertime all hands were famished; and to meet the difficulty all hands turned to, on an equal footing, and gathered wood, built fires, and cooked the meal. Afterward everything was smooth for a while; then trouble broke out between the corporal and the sergeant, each claiming to rank the other. Nobody knew which was the higher office; so Lyman had to settle the matter by making the rank of both officers equal. The commander of an ignorant crew like that has many troubles and vexations which probably do not occur in the regular army at all. However,

"IT WAS A DISAGREEABLE ANIMAL IN EVERY WAY."

with the song-singing and yarn-spinning around the camp-fire, everything presently became serene again; and by and by we raked the corn down level in one end of the crib, and all went to bed on it, tying a horse to the door, so that he would neigh if any one tried to get in.*

We had some horsemanship drill every forenoon; then,

*It was always my impression that that was what the horse was there for, and I know that it was also the impression of at least one other of the command, for we talked about it at the time, and admired the military ingenuity of the device; but when I was out West three years ago I was told by Mr. A. G. Fuqua, a member of our company, that the horse was his, that

afternoons, we rode off here and there in squads a few miles, and visited the farmers' girls, and had a youthful good time, and got an honest good dinner or supper, and then home again to camp, happy and content.

For a time, life was idly delicious, it was perfect; there was nothing to mar it. Then came some farmers with an alarm one day. They said it was rumored that the enemy were advancing in our direction, from over Hyde's prairie. The result was a sharp stir among us, and general consternation. It was a rude awakening from our pleasant trance. The rumor was but a rumor—nothing definite about it; so, in the confusion, we did not know which way to retreat. Lyman was for not retreating at all, in these uncertain circumstances; but he found that if he tried to maintain that attitude he would fare badly, for the command were in no humor to put up with insubordination. So he yielded the point and called a council of war—to consist of himself and the three other officers; but the privates made such a fuss about being left out, that we had to allow them to be present. I mean we had to allow them to remain, for they were already present, and doing the most of the talking too. The question was, which way to retreat; but all were so flurried that nobody seemed to have even a guess to offer. Except Lyman. He explained in a few calm words, that inasmuch as the enemy were approaching from

the leaving him tied at the door was a matter of mere forgetfulness, and that to attribute it to intelligent invention was to give him quite too much credit. In support of his position, he called my attention to the suggestive fact that the artifice was not employed again. I had not thought of that before.

SERGEANT BOWERS RECEIVING ORDERS.

over Hyde's prairie, our course was simple: all we had to do was not to retreat *toward* him; any other direction would answer our needs perfectly. Everybody saw in a moment how true this was, and how wise; so Lyman got a great many compliments. It was now decided that we should fall back on Mason's farm.

It was after dark by this time, and as we could not know how soon the enemy might arrive, it did not seem best to try to take the horses and things with us; so we only took the guns and ammunition, and started at once. The route was very rough and hilly and rocky, and presently the night grew very black and rain began to fall; so we had a troublesome time of it, struggling and stumbling along in the dark; and soon some person slipped and fell, and then the next person behind stumbled over him and fell, and so did the rest, one after the other; and then Bowers came with the keg of powder in his arms, whilst the command were all mixed together, arms and legs, on the muddy slope; and so he fell, of course, with the keg, and this started the whole detachment down the hill in a body, and they landed in the brook at the bottom in a pile, and each that was undermost pulling the hair and scratching and biting those that were on top of him; and those that were being scratched and bitten scratching and biting the rest in their turn, and all saying they would die before they would ever go to war again if they ever got out of this brook this time, and the invader might rot for all they cared, and the country along with him—and all such talk as that, which was dismal to hear and take part in, in such smothered, low voices, and such a grisly dark place and so wet, and the enemy maybe coming any moment.

The keg of powder was lost, and the guns too; so the growling and complaining continued straight along whilst the brigade pawed around the pasty hillside and slopped around in the brook hunting for these things; consequently we lost considerable time at this; and then we heard a sound, and held our breath and listened, and it seemed to be the enemy coming, though it could

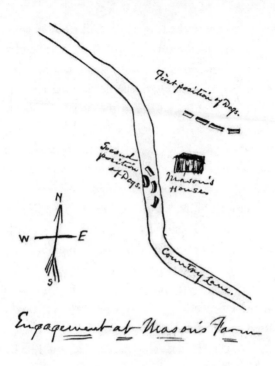

First position of Dogs.

Second position of Dogs.

Mason's House.

N

W — E

S

Country Lane.

Engagement at Mason's Farm

have been a cow, for it had a cough like a cow; but we did not wait, but left a couple of guns behind and struck out for Mason's again as briskly as we could scramble along in the dark. But we got lost presently among the rugged little ravines, and wasted a deal of time finding the way again, so it was after nine when we reached Mason's stile at last; and then before we could open our mouths to give the countersign, several dogs came bounding over the fence, with great riot and noise, and each of them took a soldier by the slack of his trousers and began to back away with him. We could not shoot the dogs without endangering the persons they were attached to; so we had to look on, helpless, at what was perhaps the most mortifying spectacle of the civil war. There was light enough, and to spare, for the Masons had now run out on the porch with candles in their hands. The old man and his son came and undid the dogs without difficulty, all but Bowers's; but they couldn't undo his dog, they didn't know his combination; he was of the bull kind, and seemed to be set with a Yale time-lock; but they got him loose at last with some scalding water, of which Bowers got his share and returned thanks. Peterson Dunlap afterwards made up a fine name for this engagement, and also for the night march which preceded it, but both have long ago faded out of my memory.

We now went into the house, and they began to ask us a world of questions, whereby it presently came out that we did not know anything concerning who or what we were running from; so the old gentleman made himself very frank, and said we were a curious breed of soldiers, and guessed we could be depended on to end up the war in time, because no government could stand the expense of the shoe-leather we should cost it trying to follow us around. "Marion *Rangers!* good name, b'gosh!" said he. And wanted to know why we hadn't had a picket-guard at the place where the road entered the prairie, and why we hadn't sent out a scouting party to spy out the enemy and bring us an account of his strength, and so on, before jumping up and stampeding out of a strong position upon a mere vague rumor— and so on and so forth, till he made us all feel shabbier than the dogs had done, not half so enthusiastically welcome. So we went to bed shamed and low-spirited; except Stevens. Soon Stevens began to devise a garment for Bowers which could be made to automatically display his battle-scars to the grateful, or conceal them from the envious, according to his occasions; but Bowers was in no humor for this, so there was a fight, and when it was over Stevens had some battle-scars of his own to think about.

Then we got a little sleep. But after all we had gone through, our activities were not over for the night; for about two o'clock in the morning we heard a shout of warning from down the lane, accompanied by a chorus from all the dogs, and in a moment everybody was up and flying around to find out what the alarm was about. The alarmist was a horseman who gave notice that a detachment of Union soldiers was on its way from Hannibal with orders to capture and hang any bands like ours which it could find, and said we had no time to lose. Farmer Mason was in a flurry this time, himself. He hurried us out of the house with all haste, and sent one of his negroes with us to show us where to hide ourselves and our tell-tale guns among the ravines half a mile away. It was raining heavily.

We struck down the lane, then across some rocky pasture-land which offered good advantages for stumbling; consequently we were down in the mud most of the time, and every time a man went down he blackguarded the war, and the people that started it, and everybody connected with it, and gave himself the master dose of all for being so foolish as to go into it. At last we reached the wooded mouth of a ravine, and there we huddled ourselves under the streaming trees, and sent the negro back home. It was a dismal and heart-breaking time. We were like to be drowned with the rain, deafened with the howling wind and the booming thunder, and blinded by the lightning. It was indeed a wild night. The drenching we were getting was misery enough, but a deeper misery still was the reflection that the halter might end us before we were a day older. A death of this shameful sort had not occurred to us as being among the possibilities of war. It took the romance all out of the campaign, and turned our dreams of glory into a repulsive nightmare. As for doubting that so barbarous an order had been given, not one of us did that.

The long night wore itself out at last, and then the negro came to us with the news that the alarm had manifestly been a false one, and that breakfast would soon be ready. Straightway we were light-hearted again, and the world was bright, and life as full of hope and promise as ever—for we were young then. How long ago that was! Twenty-four years.

The mongrel child of philology named the night's refuge Camp Devastation, and no soul objected. The Masons gave us a Missouri country breakfast, in Missourian abundance, and we needed it: hot biscuits; hot "wheat bread" prettily criss-crossed in a lattice pattern on top; hot corn pone; fried chicken; bacon, coffee, eggs, milk, buttermilk, etc.;—and the world may be confidently challenged to furnish the equal to such a breakfast, as it is cooked in the South.

We staid several days at Mason's; and after all these years the memory of the dullness, the stillness and lifelessness of that slumberous farm-house still oppresses my spirit as with a sense of the presence of death and mourning. There was nothing to do, nothing to think about; there was no interest in life. The male part of the household were away in the fields all day, the

FARMER MASON EXPLAINING THE PRINCIPLES OF WAR.

women were busy and out of our sight; there was no sound but the plaintive wailing of a spinning-wheel, forever moaning out from some distant room,—the most lonesome sound in nature, a sound steeped and sodden with homesickness and the emptiness of life. The family went to bed about dark every night, and as we were not invited to intrude any new customs, we naturally followed theirs. Those nights were a hundred years long to youths accustomed to being up till twelve. We lay awake and miserable till that hour every time, and grew old and decrepit waiting through the still eternities for the clock-strikes. This was no place for town boys. So at last it was with something very like joy that we received news that the enemy were on our track again. With a new birth of the old warrior spirit, we sprang to our places in line of battle and fell back on Camp Ralls.

Captain Lyman had taken a hint from Mason's talk, and he now gave orders that our camp should be guarded against surprise by the posting of pickets. I was ordered to place a picket at the forks of the road in Hyde's prairie. Night shut down black and threatening. I told Sergeant Bowers to go out to that place and stay till midnight; and, just as I was expecting, he said he wouldn't do it. I tried to get others to go, but all refused. Some excused themselves on account of the weather; but the rest were frank enough to say they wouldn't go in any kind of weather. This kind of thing sounds odd now, and impossible, but there was no surprise in it at the time. On the contrary, it seemed a perfectly natural thing to do. There were scores of little camps scattered over Missouri where the same thing was happening. These camps were composed of young men who had been born and reared to a sturdy independence, and who did not know what it meant to be ordered around by Tom, Dick, and Harry, whom they had known familiarly all their lives, in the village or on the farm. It is quite within the probabilities that this same thing was happening all over the South. James Redpath recognized the justice of this assumption, and furnished the following instance in support of it. During a short stay in East Tennessee he was in a citizen colonel's tent one day, talking, when a big private appeared at the door, and without salute or other circumlocution said to the colonel:

"Say, Jim, I'm a-goin' home for a few days."

"What for?"

"Well, I hain't ben there for a right smart while, and I'd like to see how things is comin' on."

"How long are you going to be gone?"

" 'Bout two weeks."

"Well, don't be gone longer than that; and get back sooner if you can."

That was all, and the citizen officer resumed his conversation where the private had broken it off. This was in the first months of the war, of course. The camps in our part of Missouri were under Brigadier-General Thomas A. Harris. He was a townsman of ours, a first-rate fellow, and well liked; but we had all familiarly known him as the sole and modest-salaried operator in our telegraph office, where he had to send about one dispatch a week in ordinary times, and two when there was a rush of business; consequently, when he appeared in our midst one day, on the wing, and delivered a military command of some sort, in a large military fashion, nobody was surprised at the response which he got from the assembled soldiery:

"Oh, now, what'll you take to *don't*, Tom Harris!"

It was quite the natural thing. One might justly imagine that we were hopeless material for war. And so we seemed, in our ignorant state; but there were those among us who afterward learned the grim trade; learned to obey like machines; became valuable soldiers; fought all through the war, and came out at the end with excellent records. One of the very boys who refused to go out on picket duty that night, and called me an ass for thinking he would expose himself to danger in such a foolhardy way, had become distinguished for intrepidity before he was a year older.

I did secure my picket that night—not by authority, but by diplomacy. I got Bowers to go, by agreeing to exchange ranks with him for the time being, and go along and stand the watch with him as his subordinate. We staid out there a couple of dreary hours in the pitchy darkness and the rain, with nothing to modify the dreariness but Bowers's monotonous growlings at the war and the weather; then we began to nod, and presently found it next to impossible to stay in the saddle; so we gave up the tedious job, and went back to the camp without waiting for the relief guard. We rode into camp without interruption or objection from anybody, and the enemy could have done the same, for there were no sentries. Everybody was asleep; at midnight there was nobody to send out another picket, so none was sent. We never tried to establish a watch at night again, as far as I remember, but we generally kept a picket out in the daytime.

In that camp the whole command slept on the corn in the big corn-crib; and there was usually a general row before morning, for the place was full of rats, and they would scramble over the boys' bodies and faces, annoying and irritating everybody; and now and then they would bite some one's toe, and the person who owned the toe would start up and magnify his English and begin to throw corn in the dark. The ears were half as heavy as bricks, and when they struck they hurt. The persons struck would respond, and inside of five minutes every man would be locked in a death-grip with his neighbor. There was a grievous deal of blood shed in the corn-crib, but this was all that was spilt while I was in the war. No, that is not quite true. But for one circumstance it would have been all. I will come to that now.

Our scares were frequent. Every few days rumors would come that the enemy were approaching. In these cases we always fell back on some other camp of ours; we never staid where we were. But the rumors always turned out to be false; so at last even we began to grow indifferent to them. One night a negro was sent to our corn-crib with the same old warning: the enemy was hovering in our neighborhood. We all said let him hover. We resolved to stay still and be comfortable. It was a fine warlike resolution, and no doubt we all felt the stir of it in our veins—for a moment. We had been having a very jolly time, that was full of horse-play and school-boy hilarity; but that cooled down now, and presently the fast-waning fire of forced jokes and forced laughs died out altogether, and the company became silent. Silent and nervous. And soon uneasy—worried—apprehensive. We had said we would stay, and we were committed. We could have been persuaded to go, but there was nobody brave enough to suggest it. An almost noiseless movement presently began in the dark, by a general but unvoiced impulse. When the movement was completed, each man knew that he was not the only person who had crept to the front wall and had his eye at a crack between the logs. No, we were all there; all there with our hearts in our throats, and staring out toward the sugar-troughs where the forest foot-path came through. It was late, and there was a deep woodsy stillness everywhere. There was a veiled moonlight, which was only just strong enough to enable us to mark the general shape of objects. Presently a muffled sound caught our ears, and we recognized it as the hoof-beats of a horse or horses. And right away a figure appeared in the forest path; it could have been made of smoke, its mass had so little sharpness of outline. It was a man on horseback; and it seemed to me that there were others behind him. I got hold of a gun in the dark, and pushed it through a crack between the logs, hardly knowing what I was doing, I was so dazed with fright. Somebody said "Fire!" I pulled the trigger. I seemed to see a hundred flashes and hear a hundred reports, then I saw the man fall down out of the saddle. My first feeling was of surprised gratification; my first impulse was an apprentice-sportsman's impulse to run and pick up his game. Somebody said, hardly audibly, "Good—we've got him!—wait for the rest." But the rest did not come. We waited—listened— still no more came. There was not a sound, not the whisper of a leaf; just perfect stillness; an uncanny kind of stillness, which was all the more uncanny on account of the damp, earthy, late-night smells now rising and pervading it. Then, wondering, we crept stealthily out, and approached the man. When we got to him the moon revealed him distinctly. He was lying on his back, with his arms abroad; his mouth was open and his chest heaving with long gasps, and his white shirt-front was all splashed with blood. The thought shot through me that I was a murderer; that I had killed a man—a man who had never done me any harm. That was the coldest sensation that ever went through my marrow. I was down by him in a moment, helplessly stroking his forehead; and I would have given anything then—my own life freely—to make him again what he had been five minutes before. And all the boys seemed to be feeling in the same way; they hung over him, full of pitying interest, and tried all they could to help him, and said all sorts of regretful things. They had forgotten all about the enemy; they thought only of this one forlorn unit of the foe. Once my imagination persuaded me that the dying man gave me a reproachful look out of his shadowy eyes, and it seemed to me that I could rather he had stabbed me than done that. He muttered and mumbled like a dreamer in his sleep, about his wife and his child; and I thought with a new despair, "This thing that I have done does not end with him; it falls upon *them* too, and they never did me any harm, any more than he."

In a little while the man was dead. He was killed in war; killed in fair and legitimate war; killed in battle, as you may say; and yet he was as sincerely mourned by the opposing force as if he had been their brother. The boys stood there a half hour sorrowing over him, and recalling the details of the tragedy, and wondering who he might be, and if he were a spy, and saying that if it were to do over again they would not hurt him unless he attacked them first. It soon came out that mine was not the only shot fired; there were five others,—a division of the guilt which was a grateful relief to me, since it in some degree lightened and diminished the burden I was carrying. There were six shots fired at once; but I was not in my right mind at the time, and my heated imagination had magnified my one shot into a volley.

The man was not in uniform, and was not armed. He was a stranger in the country; that was all we ever found out about him. The thought of him got to preying upon me every night;

I could not get rid of it. I could not drive it away, the taking of that unoffending life seemed such a wanton thing. And it seemed an epitome of war; that all war must be just that—the killing of strangers against whom you feel no personal animosity; strangers whom, in other circumstances, you would help if you found them in trouble, and who would help you if you needed it. My campaign was spoiled. It seemed to me that I was not rightly equipped for this awful business; that war was intended for men, and I for a child's nurse. I resolved to retire from this avocation of sham soldiership while I could save some remnant of my self-respect. These morbid thoughts clung to me against reason; for at bottom I did not believe I had touched that man. The law of probabilities decreed me guiltless of his blood; for in all my small experience with guns I had never hit anything I had tried to hit, and I knew I had done my best to hit him. Yet there was no solace in the thought. Against a diseased imagination, demonstration goes for nothing.

The rest of my war experience was of a piece with what I have already told of it. We kept monotonously falling back upon one camp or another, and eating up the country. I marvel now at the patience of the farmers and their families. They ought to have shot us; on the contrary, they were as hospitably kind and courteous to us as if we had deserved it. In one of these camps we found Ab Grimes, an Upper Mississippi pilot, who afterwards became famous as a dare-devil rebel spy, whose career bristled with desperate adventures. The look and style of his comrades suggested that they had not come into the war to play, and their deeds made good the conjecture later. They were fine horsemen

THE VENERABLE BLACKSMITH WITH HIS WEAPON.

and good revolver-shots; but their favorite arm was the lasso. Each had one at his pommel, and could snatch a man out of the saddle with it every time, on a full gallop, at any reasonable distance.

In another camp the chief was a fierce and profane old blacksmith of sixty, and he had furnished his twenty recruits with gigantic home-made bowie-knives, to be swung with the two hands, like the *machetes* of the Isthmus. It was a grisly spectacle to see that earnest band practicing their murderous cuts and slashes under the eye of that remorseless old fanatic.

The last camp which we fell back upon was in a hollow near the village of Florida, where I was born—in Monroe County. Here we were warned, one day, that a Union colonel was sweeping down on us with a whole regiment at his heels. This looked decidedly serious. Our boys went apart and consulted; then we went back and told the other companies present that the war was a disappointment to us and we were going to disband. They were getting ready, themselves, to fall back on some place or other, and were only waiting for General Tom Harris, who was expected to arrive at any moment; so they tried to persuade us to wait a little while, but the majority of us said no, we were accustomed to falling back, and didn't need any of Tom Harris's help; we could get along perfectly well without him—and save time too. So about half of our fifteen, including myself, mounted and left on the instant; the others yielded to persuasion and staid—staid through the war.

An hour later we met General Harris on the road, with two or three people in his company—his staff, probably, but we could not tell; none of them were in uniform; uniforms had not come into vogue among us yet. Harris ordered us back; but we told him there was a Union colonel coming with a whole regiment in his wake, and it looked as if there was going to be a disturbance; so we had concluded to go home. He raged a little, but it was of no use; our minds were made up. We had done our share;

had killed one man, exterminated one army, such as it was; let him go and kill the rest, and that would end the war. I did not see that brisk young general again until last year; then he was wearing white hair and whiskers.

In time I came to know that Union colonel whose coming frightened me out of the war and crippled the Southern cause to that extent—General Grant. I came within a few hours of seeing him when he was as unknown as I was myself; at a time when anybody could have said "Grant?—Ulysses S. Grant?—I do not remember hearing the name before." It seems difficult to realize that there was once a time when such a remark could be rationally made; but there *was*, and I was within a few miles of the place and the occasion, too; though proceeding in the other direction.

The thoughtful will not throw this war-paper of mine lightly aside as being valueless. It has this value: it is a not unfair picture of what went on in many and many a militia camp in the first months of the rebellion, when the green recruits were without discipline, without the steadying and heartening influence of trained leaders; when all their circumstances were new and strange, and charged with exaggerated terrors, and before the invaluable experience of actual collision in the field had turned them from rabbits into soldiers. If this side of the picture of that early day has not before been put into history, then history has been to that degree incomplete, for it had and has its rightful place there. There was more Bull Run material scattered through the early camps of this country than exhibited itself at Bull Run. And yet it learned its trade presently, and helped to fight the great battles later. I could have become a soldier myself, if I had waited. I had got part of it learned; I knew more about retreating than the man that invented retreating.

Mark Twain.

These notes are keyed to the text by page and line numbers: for example, 1.1 means page 1, line 1. Sources cited in the notes are referred to by the author's name and a date, or by a short title or other abbreviation. All abbreviations and short titles are expanded in the References. Works by Mark Twain are grouped there under the heading SLC. Quotations from holograph documents are transcribed verbatim from the originals (or facsimiles thereof), even when a more readily available form is cited for the convenience of the reader. Documents' locations are identified by standard Library of Congress abbreviations, all of which are defined in the References.

79.1–2 You have heard from a great many people who did something in the war] The opening sentence positions Mark Twain's paper among the other contributions to the *Century Magazine*'s series "Battles and Leaders of the Civil War," which had started to appear in November 1884; see the Introduction, pp. 47–50.

80.1 My pilot-mate was a New Yorker] The figure of Clemens's co-pilot appears to combine characteristics of the two pilot-mates who served with him on the *Alonzo Child* from September 1860 through May 1861. Horace E. Bixby (1826–1912), from Geneseo, New York, taught Clemens the craft of steamboat piloting, and during the Civil War piloted a Union gunboat. Will Bowen (1836–

93), an old friend from Hannibal, was the elder brother of Sam Bowen (for whom see pp. 118–20, note on 84.12). He was with Clemens in New Orleans on 26 January 1861, when Louisiana seceded, though Bixby was probably present as well (6 Feb 1861 to OC and MEC, *L1*, 107–16, esp. 108, 113 n. 2). As to which of them owed money to Clemens in 1861 (see the text, 80.20), they both did (*N&J1*, 61–62; *Inds*, 304–5; *L1*, 70–71; 3? Sept 1853 to Pamela A. Moffett, *L1*, 13–16 n. 8; 29 Sept 1860 to OC, *L1*, 102; 11 and 12 May 1862 to OC, *L1*, 205–13 nn. 21–22).

80.4 my father had owned slaves] Clemens's parents, John Marshall Clemens (1798–1847) and Jane Lampton Clemens (1803–90), each brought to their marriage three household slaves. All six were gradually sold off. Clemens stated that the only one he remembered was Jenny, who was a young girl when she was given to the family by Jane's grandmother. With the Clemenses she was moved from Kentucky into Tennessee, then to Florida, then Hannibal, Missouri. In 1842 or 1843 the Clemenses sold Jenny—at her request, according to Clemens—to William B. Beebe of Hannibal. In his 1905–8 notebook, Clemens wrote: "We sold slave to Beebe & he sold her down the river. We saw her several times afterward. She was the only slave we ever owned in my time" (*Inds*, 89, 327).

80.19–20 I was in the Confederate army] For an evaluation of this claim, see the Introduction, p. 27.

80.25–26 Our State was invaded by the Union forces…Jefferson Barracks] Mark Twain repeats, seemingly without irony, Governor Claiborne Jackson's claim that the presence in Missouri of United States soldiers and Union-loyal Home Guards constituted an "invasion." In his proclamation of 12 June 1861, Jackson told Missourians that the federal government's intention "to move and station its troops throughout the State whenever and wherever that might, in the opinion of its officers, be necessary" represented "the overthrow of your State government" and subjugation to "a military despotism" (U.S. Senate 1902, 263–64). This incendiary stance was derided by Unionists. "Who, or where are the invaders?" asked the St. Louis *Missouri Democrat*, noting that the federal troops "occupying" Missouri were, for the most part, citizens and residents of the state ("Unleashing the Dogs of War," 14 June 1861, 2). Mark Twain's statement that Union forces "took possession" of St. Louis and Jefferson Barracks (a United States military installation outside the city) presumably refers to the Union military build-up at those places and at the St. Louis Arsenal, between January and May 1861 (Peckham 1866, 56–57, 111, 113–14, 117–30; Scharf 1883, 1:391; New York *Times*: "Army and Navy Intelligence," 5 Mar 1861, 8; "Important from Missouri," 7 May 1861, 1; "Our St. Louis Correspondence," 12 May 1861, 2).

80.27–28 The Governor, Claib Jackson, issued his proclamation...repel the invader] Claiborne Fox Jackson (1806–62) had been elected governor of Missouri in 1860 as a "Douglas Democrat," publicly opposed to secession. But after he took office in January 1861, Jackson worked energetically for Missouri's secession. The State Assembly initially resisted his efforts to activate the state militia, and he was also prevented from gaining control of the United States Arsenal in St. Louis. In April 1861 he refused President Lincoln's requisition for Missouri troops to suppress the rebellion. After the violence at Camp Jackson on 10 May, the state assembly passed the long-stalled Military Bill, reforming the existing state militia as a State Guard loyal only to the governor. Jackson played for time, intending to build up the State Guard so that it might hold off the Union "invasion" until Confederate troops could be invited in; but negotiations came to an abrupt end on 11 June, in a contentious meeting between secessionist and Union leaders. On 12 June, from Jefferson City, Jackson issued a proclamation calling for fifty thousand volunteers. Union troops under General Nathaniel Lyon pursued, and routed Jackson's army at Boonville on 17 June. Jackson, his supporters, and his troops retreated into southwestern Missouri. The state legislature now declared the governor's seat and all state offices vacant, installing Hamilton R. Gamble as provisional governor, while Jackson presided over a secessionist shadow government at Neosho, near the Arkansas border. He spent the brief remainder of his life trying to recruit Confederate support for the cause of Missouri, dying from cancer on 6 December 1862. See also the Introduction, pp. 10–11.

81 *illus*] Mark Twain's map shows only the counties surrounding Hannibal. The area of "the Seat of War in Missouri," as mapped in *Harper's Weekly* on 6 July 1861, was much larger, taking in St. Louis, the region of the Missouri River, and Jefferson City (p. 420, and "The War in Missouri," p. 431). On Mark Twain's map, the river flowing through Ralls and Monroe counties is Salt River; the "X" between its forks presumably designates the camp of the Ralls County Rangers near Florida, Missouri.

81.4–5   Tom Lyman…was made captain] The name adapts that of Hannibal resident Tom Lyons (1835–1918), identified by Grimes as the Rangers' orderly sergeant. Lyons remained in the Missouri State Guard, then joined a Confederate artillery unit in December 1861. After the war he was a planter in Mississippi (Grimes 1886 [Appendix B, pp. 136–139]; Grimes 1926, 7; Bevier 1879, 18; Holcombe 1884, 933; "Marion Countians in the Rebel Army," Hannibal *Messenger*, 17 Nov 1861, 3).

81.6 We had no first lieutenant] According to Absalom Grimes, the company's original captain was a "William Ely," who soon deserted the outfit, and the command passed to first lieutenant Asa H. Glascock (1838–92). This may explain Clemens's recollection that the company "had no first lieutenant." In the summer of 1861 William M. Ely (1838–1911), of Ralls County, joined a regiment of the Missouri State Guard under Colonel Theodore Brace, "took part in several skirmishes but in no regular battle," and returned to his home "in the winter of 1862." In March 1862 a Hannibal newspaper noted that William M. Ely, having been "in arms against the United States Government," had taken the loyalty oath and given bond in the amount of at least $1,000 (Grimes 1886 [Appendix B, pp. 139–40]; Grimes 1926, 7–8; *Portrait*, 685–86; Williams 1913, 1:214–15; "Oath Takers," Hannibal *Messenger*, 25 Mar 1862, 2).

81.8–9 we called ourselves the Marion Rangers] The company was probably called the Ralls County Rangers; see the Introduction, p. 24.

81.11–82.26 The young fellow…Peterson Dunlap] This character is based on John L. RoBards (1838–1925), who was not, however, a member of the Ralls County Rangers or any other military company. Born in Kentucky, RoBards (whose name was spelled Robards until he changed it later in life) came to Hannibal in 1843 with his family. In 1849 he accompanied his father's expedition overland to the California gold mines, returning two years later as the much-envied "youngest forty-niner in the state of Missouri" (RoBards Scrapbooks, 1:126). His choice of a military career was thwarted by an eye injury, about which Mark Twain was skeptical: "He said he was appointed to West Point and couldn't pass because of a defect in his eye. Probably a lie. There was always a noticeable defect in his veracity" (*Inds*, 93–94). In March 1861 he finished law school at the University of Louisville; in April he married, and set up a law practice in Hannibal (*Inds*, 345–46; Stevens 1915, 4:265). For Clemens's fictionalization of him as d'Un Lap, see the Introduction, pp. 34–35.

83.1   Ed Stevens] Edmund C. Stevens (b. 1834?), Clemens's friend and classmate, became a watchmaker. Grimes says he was a steamboat pilot. In 1901 Clemens wrote: "I had a good deal of correspondence with Ed a year or two before he died.…We were great friends, warm friends, he & I. He was of a killingly entertaining spirit; he had the light heart, the care-free ways, the bright word, the easy laugh, the unquenchable genius of fun, he was a friendly light in a frowning world—he should not have died out of it" (28 Aug 1901 to John Stevens, CU-MARK; *Inds*, 349; Grimes 1886 [Appendix B, pp. 136, 141, 152).

84.6–7   Smith, the blacksmith's apprentice…of a slow and sluggish nature] In *Life on the Mississippi* Clemens recalled an apprentice blacksmith in Hannibal, a "vast, lumbering, ignorant, dull-witted lout," who became stage-struck and went to St. Louis to pursue a theatrical career. According to Clemens's 1902 notebook entry, this was Ed Buchanan (b. 1834?): "Ed. Buchanan plays Roman soldier in tin armor in St. Louis" (Notebook 45, TS p. 2, CU-MARK). Buchanan is supposed to have died around 1880, whereas "Smith" is said to have perished in the Civil War (SLC 1883, 503–6).

84.12   Jo Bowers] Clemens took the name from a comic song about a forty-niner from Pike County, Missouri, and the characterization from his Hannibal friend Samuel A. Bowen (1838?–78). Bowen's brothers Bart (1830?–68) and Will (see pp. 113–14, note on 80.1) were both steamboat pilots. Sam preceded Clemens as a pilot, and in 1858 Clemens "cubbed" under the younger man. At some point Bowen rashly and unsuccessfully married for money, a tale Clemens recounted in *Life on the Mississippi*, in his autobiographical manuscript "Villagers of 1840–3," and in his *Autobiography*. After the Missouri State Guard adventure, Bowen returned to Hannibal, where on 24 February 1862 he was arrested for being in arms against the United States. He was imprisoned at Hannibal until he consented to take an oath of loyalty, whereupon he was forced to pilot the Union steamboat *J. C. Swon*. Clemens, in Nevada, learned of this from Orion, and replied: "They have done a reckless thing, though, in putting Sam. Bowen on the 'Swon'—for if a bomb-shell happens to come his way, he will infallibly jump overboard" (11 and 12 May 1862 to OC, *L1*, 205–13). During the war, Bowen smuggled mail for the Confederacy, and after it he continued as a pilot. His last known communication with Clemens was a letter begging for fifteen or twenty dollars; Clemens annotated the envelope: "Keep this precious letter from a precious liar" (Samuel A. Bowen to SLC, 26 Apr 1876, CU-MARK). Bowen died of yellow fever on the Mississippi in 1878 and was buried at the head of island no. 65; when Clemens revisited the area in 1882 he learned that "the river has cut away the banks & Bowen is washed into the river" (*N&J2*, 561). Absalom Grimes wrote that Clemens paid for Bowen's reburial (Grimes 1886 [Appendix B, pp. 151–52). Mark Twain's disposition to portray Bowen as an oaf is tempered with nostalgic affection. In addition to being fictionalized as Jo Bowers, Bowen is the prototype of "Ben Tupper" in Mark Twain's 1877 Putnam Phalanx speech (Appendix A, pp. 129–33), and of "George Johnson" in *Life on the Mississippi* (Lomax and Lomax 1934, 421–23; *Inds*, 97, 305–6; *AutoMT1*, 402; Grimes

1926, 18–19, 77, 100, 119–20; 11 and 12 May 1862 to OC, *L1*, 205–13 and n. 22; Hannibal *Messenger*: "The Oath of Allegiance," 25 Feb 1862, 3; "Departure of the 21st from St. Louis," 22 Mar 1862, 3; "The Situation at Cairo," St. Louis *Globe-Democrat*, 14 Oct 1878, 1; "River News," Memphis *Appeal*, 6 May 1879, 3).

84.27 the Griffith place] The mansion of Dr. Robert H. Griffith (1800–64) was outside Hannibal's western boundary, on the gravel road that leads to New London in Ralls County ("Col. Bane's Acknowledgements to the Ladies," Hannibal *Messenger*, 16 Oct 1861, 2; "Watch Lost," Hannibal *Messenger*, 18 Feb 1862, 3; Fotheringham 1859, 27; National Park Service 1984, section 8; Holcombe 1884, 951).

86.12 Colonel Ralls's] John Ralls (1807–82), son of the Missouri settler for whom Ralls County was named, was a country lawyer, farmer, and Freemason. His modern biographer notes a penchant for uniforms, which "led him into wars and lodges" (Stone 1980b). He enrolled in a militia company during the Black Hawk War (1832), and, although never called into service, he was promoted to lieutenant colonel. In the Mexican War, Ralls was elected colonel of a volunteer cavalry regiment. His letters home from Mexico record more lodge activity than military action, but he was present at the battle of Santa Cruz de Rosales (16 March 1848), and came to enjoy a military reputation. In 1861 he was authorized by Governor Claiborne Jackson to recruit volunteers for the Missouri State Guard. In 1860 John Ralls owned four slaves (Grimes 1886 [Appendix B, pp. 138–39]; Campbell 1875, 464; Stone 1980a, 1980b; Grand Lodge of Missouri 1901, 27–28; Grand Lodge of Missouri 2016; *Ralls Census* 1860, 238; "Capt. John Ralls…," Palmyra [Mo.] *Weekly Whig*, 15 July 1847, 2).

86.27 Colonel Brown…at Buena Vista and Molino del Rey]
Hanceford Brown (1808–78) was a Ralls County blacksmith. Mark
Twain credits him with service at two major battles of the Mexican
War, fought in February and September 1847, respectively, but his
service has not been verified. In 1850 Brown owned four slaves
(*Ralls Census* 1850, 295; *Ralls Census* 1860, 642).

88.7 maple-sugar camp] A permanent wooden structure in
which maple sap is boiled down to make sugar.

88.10 Mason's farm] Clemens thinly disguises the name of
Enoch Griswold Matson (1787–1863), a Ralls County farmer who
had moved from Kentucky with his wife in 1816. Matson's farm
was in Spencer Township, about two miles west of New London;
in 1860 it was worked by fourteen slaves. In 1886 Grimes refers to
"Enoch G. Matson" as still alive, perhaps meaning this man's son of
the same name (1831–1912) (Grimes 1886 [Appendix B, p. 152];
Williams 1913, 1378–80; *Ralls Census* 1860, 245).

88.19 a very small mule] For Paint-Brush the mule, see the Introduction, p. 24 and n. 35.

91–92 *footnote*] when I was out West three years ago…A. G.
Fuqua] Clemens visited Hannibal in May 1882, in the course of the
Mississippi River trip that gave him material for *Life on the Mississippi*. "A. G. Fuqua" is either Andy (Anderson) Fuqua (1829–97)
or his brother Arch (b. 1833?), the sons of a Hannibal tobacconist.
Clemens was at school with both (*Inds*, 319; *AutoMT1*, 399, and
notes on pp. 610–11). Grimes mentions an "Asa Fuqua," otherwise unknown; perhaps there is some confusion with Asa Glascock,
whom he mentions elsewhere (Grimes 1926, 5).

92.8 Hyde's prairie] A section of prairie northwest of New London in Ralls County, bearing the name of a pioneer family of the region. Clemens remembered Ed and Dick Hyde, the "tough and dissipated" scions of this line, and their sister, Eliza, who "married a stranger" and moved away (*Inds*, 96, 327; "History of Hydesburg Methodist Church," MoHi, photocopy in CU-MARK; *Plat Book of Ralls County*; "Large Flock of Sheep," Hannibal *Western Union*, 7 Nov 1850, 2).

95 *illus*] Mark Twain maps the positions of the dogs using the symbol that designates the Union armies in *Personal Memoirs of U. S. Grant*:

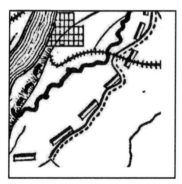

Detail of Vicksburg map showing Union forces (Grant 1885–86, 1:550).

Detail of Mark Twain's map on page 95

96.8 Yale time-lock] A lock with a built-in chronometer, which cannot be unlocked until a set time; patented in 1876.

99.2–3 plaintive wailing of a spinning-wheel...the most lone-some sound in nature] This desolating spinning-wheel seems to belong to Clemens's youthful memories of the farm-house of his uncle John A. Quarles, near Florida, Missouri; he also makes use of it in *Huckleberry Finn,* chap. 32 (*AutoMT1*, 210; *HF 2003*, 277).

100.24 James Redpath] Redpath (1833–91) was a Scottish-born journalist, abolitionist, and lecture impresario. In the 1850s he traveled in the Southern states as a correspondent for the New York *Tribune*, gathering and publishing slaves' own accounts of their bondage. He was an associate of John Brown's in the fight over slav-ery in Kansas Territory, and shortly after Brown's execution wrote the first biography of him. During the Civil War he was a news-paper correspondent with the Union army in Georgia, Tennessee, and South Carolina. In 1868 he established the Boston Lyceum Bureau, a lecture-booking agency, which featured Mark Twain as part of its roster of speakers until 1872. In May and June of 1885 Redpath, an experienced stenographer, assisted Clemens by taking down his dictations on a series of matters connected with Ulysses S. Grant (*AutoMT1,* 9–10, 66–100, and 508 n. 148.8).

100.26–27 the following instance...in East Tennessee] This an-ecdote has not been found in Redpath's published writing. He in-terviewed some Union volunteer militiamen from East Tennessee when he was in Georgia in the fall of 1864, and subsequently found himself in Tennessee, attached to the Union army of Major General George H. Thomas (Redpath 1865; McKivigan 2008, 98).

101.13 Thomas A. Harris] Born in Virginia, Thomas Alexander Harris (1826–95) moved to Missouri with his father while still a boy, and grew up near Hannibal. From an early age he thrust him-self into military affairs, serving on horseback in Missouri's Mormon

War (1838) and Iowa War (1839). He attended West Point but did not graduate. In the Mexican War he was commissioned a second lieutenant but saw no action. In 1848–49 he took part in a failed filibuster in Central America. In Hannibal, Harris was the city attorney and the editor, in 1854, of a Democratic newspaper, the *Missouri Courier*. He ran unsuccessfully for secretary of state of Missouri in 1856 as the candidate of the American Party (the "Know-Nothings"), and then successfully, as a Constitutional Unionist, for Marion County representative in 1860. In the legislature he wrote the Military Bill, which reformed the existing Missouri militia as the State Guard. With the outbreak of hostilities, Governor Jackson commissioned Harris a brigadier general in the State Guard, charging him with the organization of troops in the area north of the Missouri River. Harris commanded with distinction at the battle of Lexington (Missouri), then was appointed a representative of the "Confederate State of Missouri" in the rebel Congress at Richmond. Unseated in May 1864, he continued secret high-level work for the Confederacy, developing chemical weapons to be used against Northern shipping and civilians. After the fall of Richmond, he was arrested while fleeing to Cuba, imprisoned in Fort McHenry, then paroled and pardoned. He lived abroad, then returned to the Southern states, eventually settling in Kentucky, where he filled various state offices. A celebrated character and a polished gentleman, he was also derided as an incessant talker, "shallow, vain and frothy" ("Gen. Rains and Gen. Harris, of Missouri," New York *Times*, 13 July 1861, 4; "Change," Glasgow [Mo.] *Weekly Times*, 12 Jan 1854, 2; "Our State Ticket—Sentiment of the Country Press," St. Louis *Dispatch*, 2 May 1856, 1, reprinting the Alexandria [Mo.] *Delta* of unknown date; "Jefferson City,

March 6," St. Joseph [Mo.] *Weekly Free Democrat*, 9 Mar 1861, 2; Singer 2005, 98–112; Allardice 1995, 120–22; "Maj. Thos. A. Harris…," Glasgow [Mo.] *Weekly Times*, 14 June 1860, 3; "Reads Like Romance," Palmyra [Mo.] *Spectator*, 5 Nov 1880, 1; "Gen. Harris Dead," Louisville *Courier-Journal*, 10 Apr 1895, 7; "Yucatan Was the Prize," New York *Sun*, 13 June 1897, 16).

104.24–25 I had killed a man] On the historical status of this episode, see the Introduction, pp. 32–34.

106.24 Ab Grimes] Absalom Carlisle Grimes (1834–1911), born in Kentucky, grew up in St. Louis. His father and uncle were Mississippi River pilots, and Grimes followed the family trade from the age of fifteen. In "The Private History," Clemens distances himself from Grimes by assigning him to a different company, but comparison of their memoirs confirms that they describe one and the same outfit. Among the subjects he jotted down for "Autobiography of a Damned Fool," Clemens lists "Ab Grimes" (see p. 44). After the Ralls County Rangers disbanded, Grimes became a spy and mail smuggler for the Confederacy. Several times captured, several times escaped, and twice sentenced to death, he was pardoned by President Lincoln in 1864. After the war, Grimes returned to piloting, then moved to St. Louis, where he was successively a policeman, a private detective, and the owner of a boardinghouse. In 1882 he assisted in a prominent St. Louis man's attempt to assassinate his wife's lover. Grimes then moved to Lincoln County, where he was superintendent of a hunting club. In 1906 he shot and killed a young man who had "used insulting language" toward Grimes's twenty-year-old wife. He wrote to Clemens from the jail in Troy, Missouri, on 12 November, reminiscing about the days way back yonder in June or July 1861. Nearly 46 years ago the average lifetime of a man, when the scenes of Nuck Matsons Home—the vinegar keg Barber chair Old Col Ralls Home—Gordins [i.e., Goodwin's] Mill where Lieutenant Clemens loomed up into exhistence—the March to Head quarters in the Old Stable—the Horsetrough—which was wont to be the bed chamber of Lieut Clemens—the Ignominious return march—the *not much* Dinner at Col Tinkers—the nights camp in Col Splawns Barn & the final Disbanding of the REGIMENT next day—& return in disgrace again to Matsons Farm—& last though not least the endurance & Patience of "Paint Brush" (CU-MARK)

After being acquitted, Grimes returned to St. Louis. In 1910, with his daughter's assistance, he revised and expanded a war memoir he had begun to compose long before. The Civil War remained always at the core of his existence, and "it is related of him that he never got over his hatred of Northern men" ("Former St. Louis Policeman…," St. Louis *Post-Dispatch*, 11 Jan 1908, 2; Grimes 1886 [reprinted in this volume as Appendix B]; Grimes 1926; "Sinking of the Shamrock," Cairo [Ill.] *Evening Times*, 2 Nov 1865, 4; "The Tevis Divorce Case," Cairo [Ill.] *Bulletin*, 4 Apr 1883, 1; "Capt. A. C. Grimes, Who Killed Joe Hines at the Grimes Club Oct. 31, and His Young Wife," Elsberry [Mo.] *Democrat*, 9 Nov 1906, 1, enclosed with Grimes to SLC, 12 Nov 1906, CU-MARK; St. Louis *Post-Dispatch*: "Grimes, 'Duty Bound,' Slew Man, Is Freed," 11 Jan 1908, 2; "Capt. Grimes, at 76, to Go on the Vaudeville Stage," 8 June 1910, 8).

107.5–108.1 fierce and profane old blacksmith…twenty recruits with gigantic home-made bowie-knives] Grimes identifies the blacksmith's company as the Salt River Tigers. Clemens was right to think them a tougher outfit than his own. They raided the telegraph office at Palmyra, Missouri, in August 1861, then apparently joined the regiment of Colonel Theodore Brace and fought in the battle of Lexington in September 1861. Brace remembered the Tigers' leader as "Captain Grisby," presumably Elisha L. Grigsby (1835–1901) of Florida, Missouri, who went on to join the Confederate army, serving in the sharpshooter battalion of Lebbeus A. Pindall. Reportedly most of the Salt River Tigers were finally "killed, wounded or missing," but Grigsby survived, married his sweetheart, and became a county judge (Grimes 1886 [Appendix B, p. 138]; Grimes 1926, 7; Williams 1913, 1:214–15, 1:485; "Palmyra, Mo., Aug. 17," Muscatine [Iowa] *Weekly Journal*, 23 Aug 1861, 1; "A Document Captured from a Rebel in Ralls County," Hannibal *Messenger*, 1 Apr 1862, 2; "Confederate Soldier Writes Sweetheart from Army Camp," Mexico [Mo.] *Ledger*, 21 Mar 1951, 5).

109.2–3 I did not see that brisk young general again until last year] This meeting with Thomas A. Harris has not been documented. By 1879 Harris lived in the region of Louisville, Kentucky; Clemens lectured in Louisville on 5 and 6 January 1885, and could have seen him then. It is reported that when Clemens visited New Orleans in 1882 he sang Harris's praises and "described his happy and imperturbable philosophy under all discouragements" ("The Real Mulberry Sellers," Washington *Post*, 13 Sept 1906, 6; "Blackburn's Appointments," Hickman [Ky.] *Courier*, 22 Aug 1879, 1).

109.7–8 General Grant. I came within a few hours of seeing him] On this false claim, see the Introduction, pp. 37–38. This is not Clemens's earliest fictional brush with Grant: in *Life on the Mississippi* (chap. 25) he claims to have seen Grant "drilling his first command" at Cairo, Illinois. Grant did not arrive at Cairo until 4 September 1861.

109.25–26 There was more Bull Run material…than exhibited itself at Bull Run] In describing raw recruits as "Bull Run material," Mark Twain repeats the general estimate of the First Battle of Bull Run (21 July 1861), which blamed the rout of the Union forces on inexperienced volunteer troops. William Tecumseh Sherman, who was there, wrote that the Union forces "had good organization, good men, but no cohesion, no real discipline, no respect for authority, no real knowledge of war" (Sherman 1875, 1:181–82).

APPENDIX A

MARK TWAIN'S SPEECH AT HARTFORD, CONNECTICUT, 2 OCTOBER 1877

[Text from "Our Military Guests. The Ancients and Honorables," Hartford *Courant*, 3 October 1877, 2, with typographical errors silently emended. Mark Twain made these remarks at a banquet given by the Putnam Phalanx, a Hartford military organization, in honor of the visiting Ancient and Honorable Artillery Company of Massachusetts.]

The last time I had the privilege of breaking bread with soldiers was some years ago, with the oldest military organization in England, the Ancient and Honorable Artillery Company of London, somewhere about its six hundredth anniversary; and now I have enjoyed this privilege with its eldest child, the oldest military organization in America, the Ancient and Honorable Artillery company of Massachusetts, on this your two hundred and fortieth anniversary. Fine old stock, both of you—and if you fight as well as you feed, God protect the enemy.

I did not assemble at the hotel parlors to-day to be received by a committee as a mere civilian guest; no, I assembled at the headquarters of the Putnam Phalanx and insisted upon my right to be escorted to this place as one of the military guests. For I, too, am a soldier! I am inured to war. I have a military history.

I have been through a stirring campaign, and there is not even a mention of it in any history of the United States or of the southern confederacy—to such lengths can the envy and the malignity of the historian go! I will unbosom myself here, where I cannot but find sympathy; I will tell you about it, and appeal through you to justice.

In the earliest summer days of the war, I slipped out of Hannibal, Missouri, by night, with a friend, and joined a detachment of the rebel General Tom Harris's army (I find myself in a minority here) up a gorge behind an old barn in Ralls County; Colonel Ralls swore us in. He made us swear to uphold the flag and constitution of the United States, and to destroy any other military organization that we caught doing the same thing. In other words, we were to repel invasion. Well, you see, this mixed us. We couldn't really tell which side we were on, but we went into camp and left it to the God of Battles, (for that was the term then). I was made second lieutenant and chief mogul of a company of eleven men, for we had no captain. My friend, who was nineteen years old, six feet high, three feet wide, some distance through, and just out of the infant school, was made orderly sergeant. His name was Ben Tupper. He had a hard time. When he was mounted and on the march he used to go to sleep, and his horse would reach around and bite his leg, and then he would cry and curse, and want to go home. The other men pestered him a good deal, too. When they were dismounted they said they couldn't march in double file with him because his feet took up so much room. One night when we were around the camp fire, a fellow on the outside of the circle said, "Ben Tupper put down that newspaper—it casts a shadow like a blanket." Ben said, "I ain't got any newspaper." Then that other fellow said, "O, I see—'twas your ear!" We all slept in the corn crib, on the corn, and the rats were very thick. Ben Tupper had been rightly reared, and when he was ready for bed he would start to pray and a rat would bite him on the heel, and then he would sit up and swear all night and keep everybody awake. He was town-bred and did not seem to have any correct idea of military discipline. If I commanded him to shut up, he would say, "Who was your nigger last year?" One evening I ordered him to ride out on picket duty about three miles, to the beginning of a prairie. Said he, "What!—in the night!—and them blamed Union soldiers likely to be prowling around there any time!" So he wouldn't go. Next morning I ordered him again. Said he, "In the rain!—I think I see myself!" He didn't go. Next day I ordered him on picket duty once more. This time he looked hurt. Said he, "What! on Sunday?—you must be a dam fool!" Picketing was impracticable, so I dropped it from my military system.

We had a good enough time there at that barn, barring the rats and the mosquitoes and the rain. We levied on both parties impartially, and both parties hated us impartially. But one day we heard that the invader was approaching, so we had to pack up and move, of course. Inside of twenty-four hours he was coming again. So we moved again. Next day he was after us once more. We didn't like it much, but we moved rather than make trouble. This went on for a week or ten days more, and we saw considerable scenery. Then Ben Tupper lost patience. Said he, "War ain't what it's cracked up to be: I'm going home if I can't ever get a chance to sit down. Why do those people keep us a-humping around so? Blame their skins, do they think this is an excursion?" Some of the other town boys began to grumble: they complained that there was an insufficiency of umbrellas. So I sent around to the farmers and borrowed what I could. Then they complained that the Worcestershire sauce was out. There was mutiny and dissatisfaction all around, and of course here came the enemy pestering us again—as much as two hours before breakfast, too, when nobody wanted to turn out, of course. This was a little too much. The whole command felt insulted. I sent an aid to the brigadier, and asked him to assign us a district where there wasn't so much bother going on. The history of our campaign was laid before him, but instead of being touched by it, what did he do? He sent back an indignant message. He said, "You have had a dozen chances inside of two weeks to capture the enemy, and he is still at large. Feeling bad? Stay where you are this time, or I will court-martial and hang the whole of you." I submitted this rude message to my command, and asked their advice. Said the orderly sergeant, "If Tom Harris wants the enemy, let him come and get him; I ain't got any use for my share. And who's Tom Harris, anyway, that's putting on so many frills? Why I knew him when he wasn't nothing but a darn telegraph operator. Gentlemen, you can do as you choose; as for me I've got enough of this sashshaying around so's 't you can't get a chance to pray because the time's all required for cussing. So off goes my war-paint—you hear *me!*" The whole regiment said, "That's the talk for me!" So then and there my brigade disbanded itself and tramped off home, I at the tail of it.

I hung up my sword and returned to the arts of peace. We were the first men that went into the service in Missouri; we were the first that went out of it anywhere. This, gentlemen, is the history of the part which my division took in the great rebellion, and such is the military record of its commander-in-chief. And this is the first time that the deeds of those eleven warriors have been brought officially to the notice of mankind. Treasure these things in your hearts, and so shall the detected and truculent historians of this land be brought to shame and confusion. I ask you to fill your glasses and drink with me to the reverent memory of the orderly sergeant and those other neglected and forgotten heroes my foot-sore and travel-stained paladins, who were first in war, first in peace, and were not idle during the interval that lay between.

Absalom Grimes in Confederate uniform. Missouri Historical Society, St. Louis.

ABSALOM GRIMES: "MARK TWAIN'S CAMPAIGN."

[Grimes's letter to the editor of the St. Louis *Missouri Republican* is reprinted, with typographical errors and newspaper styling silently emended, from the issue of 4 September 1886, page 1. The letter formed part of a series entitled "Tales of the War."]

KING'S LAKE, Lincoln County, Mo., July 31. [Editor Republican.] I have read with much interest in your columns the sketches of war history written by both the boys in blue and the grey, and I thought, perhaps, you would accept an article from your humble servant. As Mark Twain is a very noted and interesting person throughout our land, I think a few remarks in regard to his war career might interest your readers, many of whom are his personal acquaintances, and some of them, I am sure, can vouch for much that I may write in regard to him, as they, like myself, were in company with him during the time referred to. I see in the December number of the New York *Century*, Mark, himself, has endeavored to give a "Private

History" of a "Campaign That Failed," but in doing so I consider his memory sadly at fault, and very many interesting events of his war record have been omitted, and other events he has not accurately described, according to my recollection.

But to my story. In the latter part of May, 1861, after the Camp Jackson fracas, I concluded I would leave the river; go to my home near New London, Ralls county, Mo., and wait until all trouble and difficulties should blow over, which I presumed would require two or three weeks. A short time after that the excitement got up to old Ralls, and one fine morning I learned a whole brigade of recruits for the rebel army had come out during the night and was quartered out at Nuck Matson's, two miles west of New London. This, with previous news, etc., had caused me to become quite enthusiastic in the Southern cause, so I went over to Matson's to review the troops there assembled in behalf of the South. I found the "brigade" to consist of about ten young men; most of them I knew, namely, Charley Mills, Jack Colter, Tom Lyon, Ed Stephens, Sam Bowen and Sam Clemens (Mark Twain) and a few others. The "brigade" was undetermined what destructive move they would make first, but on the suggestion of someone nearly all of them had their hair cut off as short as possible, so as to allow the enemy no advantage in close quarters. Tom Lyon acted as barber, with a pair of sheep-shears, in order that any hair which escaped cutting should be pulled out. This preparation on the part of the brigade inspired me so that I could no longer refrain from deciding my future course during the conflict, so I mounted the empty vinegar keg which was placed out under the shade trees and like the balance of the boys I soon had pulled out what hair the sheep-shears failed to cut, while the little niggers stood around laughing, and on being asked what they were laughing at, said: "You isn't got no mo' har den I is." After much deliberation and laying of plans in two or three days horses were provided for the "brigade" and we struck out west, as we learned the enemy would probably be in Hannibal in a few weeks and we were liable to be captured at any moment after their arrival, and we must have time to "organize" before they advanced. It would be absurd for me to undertake to describe the appearance of the brigade when mounted. I will only say no two soldiers looked alike in any respect, except, I believe, we all rode astride or straddle. I will only mention one horse especially, and that was a little yellow mule, frisky as a buck-rabbit, with long, erect ears. The mule was about four feet high, with tail sticking out on a dead level, and looked as if he had been located on the vinegar keg and Lyon had used the sheep-shears on the wrong end, for the mule's tail was shaved as with a razor within six inches of the end. Then there was a large bunch of hair left, which resembled exactly a painter's only tool. Now, on this little yellow mule was located Mark Twain, one valise, one carpet-sack, one overcoat, one pair heavy cowskin boots, one pair grey blankets, one home-made quilt, one frying-pan, one old-fashioned Kentucky squirrel rifle, twenty yards of sea-grass rope, and one umbrella. Said mule was donated to Mark Twain by Harvey Glasscock (cousin to my wife), and on account of the close resemblance of the mule's tail to a paint brush, Mark had him christened and named Paint Brush. Well, we proceeded west, until late in the evening, when we arrived at Col. Bill

Splawn's, where we took supper and remained over night. Next day the "brigade" went over to old Col. John Ralls', who gave us quite a lecture on the importance of our mission, etc., and then after stating that he was duly appointed and authorized by Gov. Jackson to recruit and swear in recruits for the Southern army, we were all sworn in, and for the first time began to realize that somebody was going to get into trouble. That afternoon we rode about five miles in a northwest direction to a place called Goodwin's Mill, which I think was located on a branch of Salt river. There we found another squad of men who had just organized a company and called themselves the Salt River Tigers. I tell you, their very appearance would have filled the enemy with "holy terror," and caused a stampede equal to Bull Run. The old blacksmith of whom Mark speaks in the *Century* had completed their war outfit by furnishing each man with a huge sabre or knife made from mowing scythes, sickle bars, long files, and goodness only knows what else. Now among the Tigers were some musicians, the Bros. Martin and two others. While visiting this camp and seeing the Tigers drawn up in line, answer at roll call, it occurred to someone of the brigade that we ought to have someone to take command, give orders, be able to make some kind of a military appearance, etc., and after making a few remarks it was moved and seconded we elect officers, and as the brigade did not have sufficient men to elect all the generals necessary, with full quota of colonels, lieutenant-colonels, majors, chiefs different staffs, surgeons, quartermasters, commissaries, etc., we decided to commence and elect only company officers, and if there was any left, we could then commence with them and fill the vacant offices before mentioned, beginning from the commissary and go up, as we would be more likely to need the commissary officers first. The nominations for captain were Wm. Ely and Asa Glasscock. The former winning in a few "cold decks" and beating Glasscock. Then Glasscock was unanimously elected first lieutenant, Sam Bowen (the man whom Mark Twain refers to as Sergt. Bowers) then nominated Sam Clemens (Mark Twain) for second lieutenant. He was elected unanimously in a few seconds. Bowen was then made a sergeant, and Tom Lyon orderly sergeant. It was all the same to us. We didn't know the difference. After the election was over and all officers elected, with three or four left to act as privates, we called on our second lieutenant, Mark Twain, for a "speech! speech!" After some hesitancy in so large a crowd (the Tigers also being present) he mounted the end of an old log and blushingly said: "You'd scarce expect one of my age to speak in public on the—this log. Well, boys, I thank you for electing me your lieutenant; I will try and do my duty and the square thing by you all. But—hell, I can't make you a speech," and down he got, amidst the cheers and hurrahs of the entire command. Capt. Ely then commanded us to meet next morning in a certain prairie for drill, as there were no fields or meadows in the neighborhood large enough (although some contained sixty acres or more). We then dispersed—going in different directions to the different farmhouses for grub and to stay over night. Myself and others went to Mr. Washington Clayton's. Next morning before going to the prairie we assembled at Col. John Ralls'. And now for the sword of Buena Vista and Molino del Rey, of which Mark speaks.

When I left New London old Col. Hanceford Brown gave me an old sword and belt that he had used in the Mexican war and I believe his father had carried in the war of 1812 and which was an old family relic. Well, while at Col. Ralls', I concluded our second lieutenant ought to have a sword and as I was a pilot on the Upper Mississippi and he a pilot on the Lower Mississippi we were acquainted long before we met at Matson's, so I concluded he should have the sword and requested Col. Ralls to make the presentation speech. This he did and Lieut. Clemens responded, but I do not remember his words. We then repaired to the prairie, drew up in line and waited for Capt. Ely to show up—which he never did from that day to this, so far as I know. Lieut. Glasscock then assumed command of the Ralls County Rangers, that being the name our company adopted, and we then retired to a secluded camp on Salt river, somewhere in the edge of Monroe county, close by a one-story log farmhouse—I do not remember the farmer's name, but I guess the same one that Mark refers to as Farmer Mason. After we had been in this camp about two days we were joined by another company, among whom was Burr McPherson of Hannibal, Mo., who acted as kind of boss and drill-master. There was not such a thing as a tent in existence for all we knew, so we cut sticks and stuck them in the ground and spread some of our blankets and quilts over the top, and as for grub, the most important part of the whole business, it had very little to do with that camp. We had a skillet or two, a few fryingpans. I remember seeing a twenty-five pound sack of flour at one time, but how it got there I don't know. The boys used to go out foraging and bring in cornmeal, fat side meat and occasionally sorghum. That constituted our entire bill of fare during the time we remained there, which was about two weeks, and during our stay it rained nearly every day or night, so that Salt river became bank full. Near, or in our camp, was located the log stable belonging to the farmhouse, and which stable was used as headquarters. A room or apartment was at each end and a gangway or passway between about twelve or fifteen feet wide all covered with clapboard roof, and in this gangway or passage we used to cook on account of the rain. Along on one side was a large horse-trough to feed in, and in which Lieut. Clemens used to sleep. The next day or so after going into camp the news came by someone that the Yankee army was coming out from Hannibal in full force, and would leave the railroad at Monroe City and march on our camp. The news created much excitement and it was quickly decided to put out pickets. Sam Bowen, Ed Stephens and myself were selected as the most reliable men, as we were all pilots and could keep awake better than the other boys. Mark Twain, our lieutenant, was placed in command of the squad, and we started about dark for our post, which was about two miles north, and at the mouth of a lane leading toward Monroe City. Opposite the mouth of said lane were some trees and bushes, where we tied our horses, and then shook up some dimes in a hat in order to see who should stand first, second and third watch, as we did not deem it necessary for all of us to lose our rest all the time. The first watch fell to Sergt. Bowen, second to myself and third to Ed Stephens. Bowen stood at the mouth of the lane from 8 p.m. to 11. I took his place to remain until 3 a.m., but at 1 a.m. I heard the enemy coming and went over and waked up the other boys. Lieut. Clemens mounted Paint Brush and held our horses while we all went across to the mouth of the lane to watch the movements of the enemy. I stood first and so commanded the view. Presently I saw them raise the hill and swerve from right to left, and at the same time raised my double-barreled shotgun and let go both barrels into their ranks, and without remaining to see how many were killed we turned and struck out for our horses. To our horror, our lieutenant was over a hundred yards off and still going, and we halooing for him to stop, and finally Sam Bowen levelled his old shotgun and said, "D– – you, Sam, if you don't stop, I'll let her go!" So Sam halted, and when we came up Bowen [was] still cursing him. Mark says, "J—! Paint Brush got so excited I couldn't hold him in!" So we got mounted, and away we went at full speed for camp, leaving our lieutenant and Paint Brush far in the rear, and last we heard of him he was saying, "H– – –, you want the Yanks to capture me." When we reached camp the boys were all up and in line, in all sorts of rigs—a coat and a pair of shoes, hat and pair of pants, shirt and pair of socks, shirt and coat; hat, shirt and one boot, and some in Chinese rig, and on being told the cause of the firing, waited breathlessly for the approach of the Yanks. Presently there was a clatter of hoofs heard coming down the ravine, and the order was given to "make ready," when we happened to think of our lieutenant and Paint Brush, and called to Commander Burr McPherson for God's sake to hold fire for a few moments, as it must be our lieutenant coming. And so it was. We drew a sigh of relief as he came full tilt, and never even tried to check Paint

Brush until he got to the far end of the line, and then, you bet, the picket guard heard from him. Among other abuses we got was one for the loss of his hat. We stood in that line, momentarily expecting the enemy, until daylight, when all retired in good order. After an apology for breakfast, I requested Sergt. Bowen to go with me back to the mouth of the lane, to see if the enemy had removed their dead. On arriving there, I cautiously approached the fence corner and took in the situation, and in a few moments I said: "Sam, I want to tell you something, but you must swear you will not reveal it to any human being as long as you and I both shall live."

Sam says: "I'll swear and cross my heart."

Said I: "Do you see those large mullen stalks there on the side of that hill?"

"Yes."

"Well, last night the wind must have blown and caused them to move, for I would have sworn they were Feds on horse-back."

"Well, you d— fool, you played —, didn't you?" was his only remark; but en route to camp he soon became jovial again and joked about the lieutenant and "Paint Brush." But the very first thing Sam did on our arrival in camp was to give the whole thing away, and I was hourly reminded of those mullen stalks for several days. Mark Twain refers to a "man that was killed in camp one night," the circumstances are these: One dark, rainy night (I think the very next night after I fired on the mullen stalks), a good-natured fellow (but a hard case), by the name of Dave Young—who was always about three-thirds full of whiskey— was placed on camp guard. During the night many of us were awakened by heavy tramping and presently we heard the guard say "halt you! Ain't you going to halt and give the pass-word?" The tramping still continued, which, with the order of the guard, had aroused a good many of the boys, when the guard cried again: "Halt or I'll shoot," and bang, bang went both barrels of his gun. A heavy fall and a groan, and up and out into the dark all hands rushed, and to the place from whence preceded the groans, and there lay in the agonies of death an old gray horse, the property of Dave Young (the guard), himself, who was standing over him looking quite sad. That was the only killing I ever knew of in that camp—or while Mark was in the army. By this time Mark had become sorely afflicted with a boil, and it was a source of much comfort to him that there were no chairs or stools in camps for him to sit on, for if there had been such would have been very antagonistic to that boil. Therefore Mark had a lot of straw put in the large trough in the passageway of the stable, and soon spent all of his time holding the straw down, and wondering at the great amount of patience possessed by Job in olden times. For a few days nothing of interest occurred to enthuse the troops to any extent, the grub began to get thinner every day, and we began to get discouraged and to "thirst for blood." The talk, of moving camp, advancing on the enemy, tearing up the railroad tracks and firing into cars containing Yanks, became general, among a great many of us, but these topics and plans were much disapproved of by Commander Burr McPherson and Lieut. Clemens, who said "Gen. Tom Harris has been appointed to this district and division of the army and he will soon be here and lead us on to victory or death." About that time we learned that Tom Harris had been stopping up at Clay Price's, only two miles away, for a week, living on the fat of the land while we were in the rain, wet and swamp, chewing sowbelly and corn bread. So that settled the case, and many of us began packing up our traps, intending to advance on Monroe City at all hazards. Mark was lying in the old horse trough wrecked by his boil, and remonstrating with us about thus breaking up camp, and showing no military discipline after all our teachings, etc. We told him we were in for blood and railroad iron, and were going on the war-path. As we were about to depart he raised up on one elbow and said, "Well, boys, if you are determined to go, it's no use for me to try and hold this posish by myself, so, Ab, if you will saddle up old Paint Brush, I'll jine the army and go along." So I saddled up "Paint Brush," put all of Mark's traps on him and led him beside the trough, and our lieutenant rolled out onto him. It was but a few steps to Salt river, which we had to cross, but Paint Brush refused to "take water," and after much persuasion Mark says: "Well, Ab, I guess I'll have to get you to lead Paint Brush in, he won't go for me." I tied one end of an inch seagrass rope I had about the mule's neck and then took a turn around the pommel of my saddle. After some manoeuvering we got the mule close to the edge of the bank, and while smelling the water, as if to get a drink, I gave my horse the spurs, and he made a jump far out into the stream, bringing Paint Brush along. The top of the bank where we started in was only about a foot above the water, and the water eight or ten feet deep the first jump. On the opposite side the road came out gradually between two small hills. My horse swam vigorously for the other bank. I looked back over my shoulder to see how Mark and Paint Brush were getting along, but, to my horror, neither one was in sight, and I thought them both drowned, but hurried over, as I knew my seagrass rope was good for the mule. I soon landed safe, and after a few steps in the edge of the water the top of Mark's old slouch black hat, then Mark and the mule in turn showed up. As he slowly waded up out of the water the mule was very weak and weaving from side to side, and when fully out of the water Mark rolled off the mule on to the side of the bank; took off his hat, took a handkerchief out of his pocket, wrung the water out of it and slowly and solemnly wiped his face. Then looking up at me, he said in a low and solemn tone: "Ab, what do you think?"

"I think, Sam, you are pretty wet. What do you think?"

"Don't you think that mule waded every step of the way across that river?"

"Well, Sam, I think he did first rate to do that with you and that 150 pounds of luggage in ten feet of water."

"Well, it was a pretty good load for 'Paint Brush,' but it fixed to washed all the wind out of me, sure."

The boys had all waited to see Sam and the mule cross, so he slowly and carefully mounted his mule, and we proceeded on our journey. No one knew or cared where we were going, but we were headed east again. We had not proceeded very far when we met Gen. Tom Harris, whom but few of us had ever seen before, but I think Mark Twain was acquainted with him. He first ordered us back, but we only laughed at the assumed authority of a stranger to us. Then he requested us to turn and go back to camp, but it was no go. Then he begged us, but the remembrance of that camp, the sowbelly and corn bread we had chewed up was enough for us, so we rode on and went to Clay Price's ourselves, where we were served with a good breakfast, and then proceeded on our journey east. On our journey many were the jokes passed and yarns told of our campaign, so far as it went, and among other jokes, etc., Mark came in for several.

The day grew quite warm as we proceeded on our way, and about 3 o'clock in the afternoon, tired and hungry, we stopped at a nice looking two-story brick house on the right hand side, 100 or so yards off the main road. We all tied our horses and went in. On entering no one was in sight. Some of the boys took seats, while others stood about. Presently in came a thin, spare made, tall woman, with cold, gray eyes, light hair all combed back tight, and in sharp tone said:

"What do you men want?"

Her very looks and tone of voice caused some of the boys to rise and start slowly for the front door.

Mark Twain acted as spokesman and said:

"Madam, we are very tired and hungry, and we would like to get something to eat."

"Get something to eat, would you? Well, you wont get it here."

"We are willing to pay for it, madam."

"Pay nothing. Get yourselves out of here and that pretty quick or I'll make you," and reaching back of her near the head of a bed she clamped on to a large hickory stick, used to beat up a feather bed, and started for Mark.

"Hold on, madam, don't be so fast. Let's reason this case. We're gentlemen and intend to pay for all we get."

"Do you secesh pretend to call yourselves gentlemen? Get out of here. Do you think I'm going to feed rebs and my husband a colonel in the Union army? Get out."

By this time all the boys were out and getting mounted, while I remained just in the rear of Mark as he slowly advanced backward toward the front door, fearing to turn around and expose his boil to the attacks of the woman and her club. She was striking at his shins all the time, which kept him bent nearly double, all the time remonstrating with her about being so hasty, and she abusing rebs and secesh. After backing him out of the door and a few feet in the yard she "let up" with the club, but her tongue still kept on the warpath. After we were clear of her I said: "Sam, why didn't you take your pistol or sword to her?"

"Do you think I'd disgrace my sword by spilling the blood of a woman? But I believe she would just as soon hit me as not if I hadn't kept getting out of her way."

So we mounted and soon came up with the other boys who were roaring with laughter and Sam's boil was forgotten in the many remarks as to the battle of the Yankee woman and the lieutenant. We soon met a man in the road and asked him who lived back there in that next brick house.

"Col. Tinker."

"Who is Col. Tinker?"

"Why, he has been a colonel in the Yankee army three months."

"Well, who's that woman there?"

"Why, that's Mrs. Tinker. She's colonel or general at home."

"Well, I should remark she was," said Sam, and we rode on. 'Twas about 1 o'clock at night when we arrived at Col. Bill

Splawn's place again, tired, hungry and dusty. Owing to the late hour we would not disturb the family by asking for anything to eat. So we put our horses away and fed them in the large barn, and all of us got up in the loft on the hay to sleep till morning. Mark Twain selected a spot near the door in the gable end of the building. I lay but a short distance from him. Shortly after we had dropped off to sleep some one at the top of his voice yelled, "Fire!" "Fire!" Every fellow was up in an instant, and sure enough a nice little fire was just beginning to open up in the hay. Mark Twain made about two or three rolls over and out of the door. He went down on to the rocks below, a drop of about ten or twelve feet, and in doing so he sprained his ankle and sat groaning and rubbing his ankle with one hand while with the other he was feeling around for his boil, and while in said predicament the boys in the loft were busy rolling up the hay where the fire was and rolled it out the same door Mark had rolled, and down on top of him the roll of burning hay fell. I shall never forget the ludicrous scene Mark and the hay presented. Away he went down the slope on all fours—his hands and feet—with the burning hay on his back, reminding me of how we used to, when a boy, put a big coal of fire on a terrapin's back in order to see him run. Several of us stood in the door and screamed with laughter. In a moment or so the burning hay fell off his back, and was soon nothing but smoking fragments. While Mark turned his attention to us, with language that would not do to publish, myself and others went down to him, and tried to console him, and helped him into the stable below, all the while nearly choking to death, endeavoring to smother our laughter.

There was no more sleep till morn. One of the boys had gone to sleep with an old pipe in his mouth, and by so doing caused the fire and the sad results to our second lieutenant. Early in the morning we advanced in force on the house. Col. Bill Splawn's house was always open to the boys and his wife and family took great pleasure and delight in supplying our wants, which were many, and no doubt all the boys who are living always remember the kind treatment they always got there. After we had gotten our breakfast and related to Col. Bill all our exploits since we first stopped with him we started on our journey east again toward New London, which was ten miles or so away. In the afternoon we again "fetched up" at Nuck Matson's with our hair about an inch longer than it was when we left there, but we were still recognized as the same "gang." Nuck had his own time making sport of our grand campaign and safe return without the loss of a man, although our lieutenant was sadly wounded. He was put to bed and tenderly cared for by Nuck and his more than kind wife, who is now numbered among the angels in heaven. At Nuck Matson's we all disbanded and took different directions, leaving our second lieutenant there. The last I saw of him he lay groaning in bed with foot propped up, and with the amount of wrappings it looked like a baby elephant. I was told by Mrs. Matson years afterward that Sam was laid up there for a long time, and they got a crutch and a cane for him, and that they kept a little nigger on picket all the time down at the mouth of the lane, where it connected with the main road, one-fourth of a mile from the house, and oftentimes the little nigger would be seen running for dear life towards the house, which was a signal for Sam to grab his crutch and stick and break for the bushes in the woods pasture adjoining the yard. By the time the little nig would yell, "Miss Mary, de Yanks is comin'! de Yanks is comin'!" Sam would be in his hiding place, and there to remain until notified, "Mars Sam, Yanks all done gone." She said she believed the path was there still as she was relating to me the sad end of Mark Twain's war career. I never heard what became of "Paint Brush." But when Sam left there I believe he went to Keokuk and went to California with his brother, and on said journey West he wrote his first book. I have never seen Mark since, although I would like to very much. I have had one or two short letters from him and also been kindly presented with his works, "Tom Sawyer" and sketches. After I left Matson's, I went to see "my girl" once more, and then went to Paris, Mo., where I joined the Paris boys and Capt. Theo. Brace's company and went west again. My war experience terminated December 10, 1864, at which time I was representing the confederacy and located at the lower state house in Jefferson City. I believe they called it the penitentiary at the time, and it still bears the same name.

After our disbanding at Matson's, poor Sam Bowen, our sergeant, was arrested by the Feds and put into the stockade at Hannibal, and learned the trade of sawing wood; his two bosses stood one on each side, and every time Sam looked around to see if they were on hand, he looked into a big musket with a soldier on the far end; he said that was the only thing that induced him to learn the trade. He died years afterward with the yellow-fever while piloting on the steamer Mollie Moore, and was buried on the river bank which gradually washed and caved away until the coffin became exposed, and I understand the same was called to the attention of Mark Twain during one of his visits from New Orleans to St. Louis, and he persuaded the Pilot's association to have his remains removed to a place of safety and decently interred, he defraying all the expenses. I do not remember whatever became of Ed Stephens.

Enuch G. Matson's post-office address is New London, Ralls county, Mo. Asa Glasscock's address is the same place; both are "well-to-do" farmers, and can vouch for the little sketch I have given you of Mark Twain's war record. Yours respectfully,

A. C. GRIMES.

"The Private History of a Campaign That Failed" does not present a difficult textual situation. The manuscript that served as printer's copy is lost—destroyed, presumably, in the course of printing from it. The text of the *Century* printing (Cent) must certainly embody the magazine's changes to the "accidentals"—the spelling and punctuation—as opposed to the "substantives," or wording. As Cent is our sole source of the text, the intrusion of editorial house styling cannot generally be undone.

There are two limited exceptions. An autograph manuscript leaf (MS), in the library of Washington University, St. Louis, apparently belongs to an unrevised draft of "The Private History"; yet its text runs parallel, in part, to Cent, and so far as it does the present edition adopts its accidentals. The leaf's substantive variants are rejected, on the assumption that the published text incorporates Mark Twain's revisions on a lost intervening document. (Two other manuscript leaves, unlocated but available in facsimile, contain no text that runs parallel to Cent.) Secondly, information about the *Century Magazine*'s treatment of copy is furnished by the textual apparatus in the Mark Twain Project edition of *Adventures of Huckleberry Finn* (*HF 2003*). In 1884–85 the *Century* printed extracts from the forthcoming novel, using printed book pages as copy; wherever the *Century* can be seen to have altered its copy to a usage atypical of Clemens, it is plausible, in editing "The Private History," to restore his typical forms.

The placement of one illustration has been altered. The *Century Magazine* was printed in signatures, each of which used one of two kinds of paper: an uncoated stock suitable for regular text, and a coated stock that showed illustrations to advantage. As laid out in the magazine, "The Private History" took up an eight-page signature of coated paper and ran over onto four pages of an uncoated signature. If E. W. Kemble's picture "The Venerable Blacksmith with His Weapon" had been placed near the text it illustrates, it would have been the only illustration within a signature mostly given over to Henry James's (unillustrated) *The Bostonians*, so the editors moved it forward into the coated signature, altering the caption to refer readers to the relevant text. We have moved the illustration to its natural place in the narrative and adjusted the caption.

"The Private History" was originally going to be republished in the Century Company's book *Battles and Leaders of the Civil War* (Johnson and Buel 1887–89); for the circumstances of its non-appearance there, see the Introduction, pp. 69–71. Its first publication in book form was in the collection *Merry Tales* (SLC 1892), published by Clemens's own firm of Charles L. Webster and Company; Clemens, then living abroad, did no more than consent to this publication. *Merry Tales* reprinted Cent, omitting the illustrations (and, by accident, eleven words of the text, an error carried forward in subsequent reprintings). Clemens's intention to suppress the satire on John RoBards (see the Introduction, pp. 69–70) was rescinded or more probably forgotten. In 1896 the bulk of *Merry Tales*, including "The Private History," was absorbed into a catch-all volume in Harper and Brothers' Uniform Edition of Mark Twain's Works, *The American Claimant, and Other Stories and Sketches* (SLC 1896). The text of "The Private History" printed in that volume incorporates new, deliberate, and non-authorial variants—changes to spelling and punctuation, modernizations (e.g., "whilst" altered to "while"), and fussy grammatical corrections. Most of these would pass into later collected editions. The variant readings of those republications are not reported here.

In the apparatus entries below, notations like 'south-|eastern' represent a compound word broken over a line-ending. Mark Twain's insertions in manuscript are shown between carets, thus: '∧the future∧'. Readings marked "(MTP)" are emendations by the Mark Twain Project editor.

Witnesses:

Cent   "The Private History of a Campaign That Failed." *The Century Illustrated Monthly Magazine* 31, 193–204. Three copies in CU-MARK have been used.

MS   MS leaf numbered 94½, including text corresponding to 'I came…other direction.' (109.7–13); in MoSW.

Emendations and rejected variants:

85.1   south-eastern (MTP) • south-|eastern (Cent)

89.27–28   horse-troughs (MTP) • horse-|troughs (Cent)

94.22   maybe (MTP) • [*Emended on the basis of the* Century Magazine*'s treatment of copy for* Adventures of Huckleberry Finn; *see* HF 2003, *historical collation at 55.13 and twenty-two other places*]

98.12   light-hearted (MTP) • lighted-hearted (Cent)

101.4   ben (MTP) • b'en (Cent) [*Emended on the basis of the* Century Magazine*'s treatment of copy for* Adventures of Huckleberry Finn; *see* HF 2003, *historical collation at 134.26, 150.16, 150.24, and 154.22*]

101.13   A. (MTP) • H. (Cent)

104.6   horseback (MTP) • horse-|back (Cent)

107 *illus*   WEAPON (MTP) • WEAPON. (see page 203.) (Cent) [*This figure has been moved from its location in Cent nearer to the passage it illustrates; see the discussion on p. 154*]

109.5–7   In time…General Grant. (Cent) • That colonel was ∧the future∧ Gen. Grant, though I did not know it at the time. But I would not have staid, anyway, even if I had known it. (MS)

109.9   said (MS) • said, (Cent)

109.9   Grant?—I (MS) • Grant? I (Cent)

109.12   a few (Cent) • 3 (MS)

109.13   the occasion, too; (MTP) • ∧the∧ occasion, too;
         (MS); the occasion too, (Cent)

Allardice, Bruce S. 1995. *More Generals in Gray*. Baton Rouge: Louisiana State University Press.

AutoMT1. 2010. *Autobiography of Mark Twain, Volume 1*. Edited by Harriet Elinor Smith et al. The Mark Twain Papers. Berkeley and Los Angeles: University of California Press.

AutoMT3. 2015. *Autobiography of Mark Twain, Volume 3*. Edited by Benjamin Griffin, Harriet Elinor Smith, et al. The Mark Twain Papers. Berkeley and Los Angeles: University of California Press.

Bainton, George, comp. and ed. 1890. *The Art of Authorship: Literary Reminiscences, Methods of Work, and Advice to Young Beginners, Personally Contributed by Leading Authors of the Day*. New York: D. Appleton and Co.

Bates, Allan. 1964. "The Quintus Curtius Snodgrass Letters: A Clarification of the Mark Twain Canon." *American Literature* 36 (March): 31–37.

Bevier, R. S. 1879. *History of the First and Second Missouri Confederate Brigades. 1861–1865. And, From Wakarusa to Appomattox, a Military Anagraph*. St. Louis: Bryan, Brand and Co.

Bofinger, John N. 1877. "Gleanings from Our Exchanges." Cincinnati *Commercial*, 19 June 1877, unknown page, reprinting the St. Louis *Times* of unknown date. Clipping in Scrapbook 1 (1877–78), OOxM. Photocopy in CU-MARK.

Branch, Edgar Marquess. 1986. "A Proposed Calendar of Samuel Clemens's Steamboats, 15 April 1857 to 8 May 1861, with Commentary." *Mark Twain Journal* 24 (Fall): 2–27.

Brewer, David J., ed. 1902. *Crowned Masterpieces of Literature That Have Advanced Civilization: As Preserved and Presented by the World's Best Essays, from the Earliest Period to the Present Time. Vol. 10.* St. Louis: Ferd. P. Kaiser.

Briggs, Joshua Ely, and Ruth Flowerree. 1939. *A Pioneer Missourian.* Boston: Christopher Publishing House.

Burkhardt, Patrick. 2011. "The Lost Cause Ideology and Civil War Memory at the Semicentennial: A Look at the Confederate Monument in St. Louis." *Confluence* 2 (Spring/Summer): 16–25.

Campanella, Richard. 2015. "The St. Louis and the St. Charles: New Orleans' Legacy of Showcase Exchange Hotels." *Preservation in Print* 42 (April): 16–17.

Campbell, R. A., comp. 1875. *Campbell's Gazetteer of Missouri.* Revised edition. St. Louis: R. A. Campbell.

Chadwick-Joshua, Jocelyn. 1998. *The Jim Dilemma: Reading Race in* Huckleberry Finn. Jackson: University Press of Mississippi.

Clemens, Cyril, ed. 1945. "Three Mark Twain Letters." *Mark Twain Quarterly* 7 (Summer–Fall): 24.

Clemens, Will M. 1892. *Mark Twain: The Story of His Life and Work; A Biographical Sketch.* San Francisco: The Clemens Publishing Company.

Clemens, Samuel Langhorne. See SLC.

CofC. 1969. *Clemens of the "Call": Mark Twain in San Francisco*. Edited by Edgar M. Branch. Berkeley and Los Angeles: University of California Press.

Cohn, Henry S. 2015. "Mark Twain and Joseph Roswell Hawley." *Mark Twain Journal* 53 (Fall): 67–84.

Collins, Charles, comp. 1864–65. *Mercantile Guide and Directory for Virginia City, Gold Hill, Silver City and American City....*Virginia City, Nev.: Printed for Agnew and Deffebach.

Coryell, Irving. 1937. "Josh, of the 'Territorial Enterprise.'" *North American Review* 243 (Summer): 287–95.

Cox, James M. 1966. *Mark Twain: The Fate of Humor.* Princeton: Princeton University Press.

CtHMTH. Mark Twain House and Museum, Hartford, Conn.

CtY-BR. Yale University, Beinecke Rare Book and Manuscript Library, New Haven, Conn.

CU-MARK. University of California, Mark Twain Papers, The Bancroft Library, Berkeley.

DeHaven, Mary Dobyns. 1913. "Reminiscences of War Times." In *Reminiscences of the Women of Missouri During the Sixties*. N.p.: Missouri Division, United Daughters of the Confederacy.

Dempsey, Terrell. 2003. *Searching for Jim: Slavery in Sam Clemens's World.* Columbia: University of Missouri Press.

Denslow, Ray V. 1924. "Mark Twain, a Missouri Mason." *Missouri Grand Lodge Bulletin* 1 (May): 53–60.

Doten, Alfred. 1973. *The Journals of Alfred Doten, 1849–1903.* Edited by Walter Van Tilburg Clark. 3 vols. Reno: University of Nevada Press.

ET&S1. 1979. *Early Tales and Sketches, Volume 1 (1851–1864).* Edited by Edgar Marquess Branch and Robert H. Hirst, with the assistance of Harriet Elinor Smith. The Works of Mark Twain. Berkeley, Los Angeles, London: University of California Press.

Eutsey, Dwayne. 2018. "'Alas, Poor Mark!': The Masonic Response to Mark Twain's Rebuke of Freemasonry as 'Foolishness.'" *Mark Twain Journal* 56 (Spring): 121–23.

Fatout, Paul. 1976. *Mark Twain Speaking.* Iowa City: University of Iowa Press.

Fellman, Michael. 1989. *Inside War: The Guerrilla Conflict in Missouri During the American Civil War.* New York: Oxford University Press.

Field, Eugene. 1885. "Sharps and Flats." Chicago *News*, 21 December, 2.

Fishkin, Shelley Fisher.
    1993. *Was Huck Black? Mark Twain and African-American Voices.* New York: Oxford University Press.
    1997. *Lighting Out for the Territory: Reflections on Mark Twain and American Culture.* New York: Oxford University Press.

Fitch, Tom. 1910. "Tom Fitch on Mark Twain." *Los Angeles Times*, 24 April, part 5, 23.

Fotheringham, H. 1859. *Hannibal City Directory, for 1859–60.* Hannibal, Mo.: H. Fotheringham.

Fulton, Joe B. 2010. *The Reconstruction of Mark Twain: How a Confederate Bushwhacker Became the Lincoln of Our Literature.* Baton Rouge: Louisiana State University Press.

Gardner, Charles, comp. 1861. *Gardner's New Orleans Directory for 1861.* New Orleans: Charles Gardner.

Gerber, John. 1955. "Mark Twain's 'Private Campaign.'" *Civil War History* 1 (March): 37–60.

Grand Lodge of Missouri.
    1869. *Proceedings of the Forty-Ninth Annual Communication of the M. W. Grand Lodge, A.F. and A.M....*St. Louis: [Grand Lodge of Missouri].
    1901. *Biographies and Engravings of Grand Masters, Grand Treasurers and Grand Secretaries of the Grand Lodge of Missouri. From 1821 to 1900, Inclusive.* N.p.: n.p.
    2016. "Missouri Masonic Museum: The Ralls Exhibit." *The Freemason* 6 (Spring): 12–13.

Grant, Ulysses S.
    1885–86. *Personal Memoirs of U. S. Grant.* 2 vols. New York: Charles L. Webster and Co.
    1969. *The Papers of Ulysses S. Grant, Volume 2: April–September, 1861.* Edited by John Y. Simon. Carbondale: Southern Illinois University Press.

Grimes, Absalom C.

  1876. "Memoir of Mark Twain." Terre Haute (Ind.) *Evening Gazette*, 19 February, 2, reprinting the St. Louis *Journal* of unknown date. Another reprint is in the Shelbina (Mo.) *Democrat*, 15 March 1876, 2.

  1877. "River News." Cincinnati *Gazette*, 19 January, 7, reprinting the Memphis *Avalanche* of unknown date. Another reprint is in the Hannibal *Clipper*, 22 January 1877, 4.

  1879. "Ab. Grimes. The Old Patrolman…." New Orleans *Times-Picayune*, 1 September, 3. Reprinted "almost in full" in Scharf 1883, 419–21.

  1886. "Tales of the War. Ab Grimes Retells the Story of Mark Twain's Campaign." St. Louis *Missouri Republican*, 4 September 1886, 1. Reprinted in this volume as Appendix B.

  1926. *Absalom Grimes, Confederate Mail Runner*. Edited from Captain Grimes' Own Story by M. M. Quaife, of the Burton Historical Collection. New Haven: Yale University Press.

Hall, Edward P., and John W. Bixler, eds. 1897. *Decisions of the Department of the Interior in Appealed Pension and Bounty-Land Claims. Volume 8*. Washington, D.C.: Government Printing Office.

Hardy, John. 1879. *Selma: Her Institutions, and Her Men*. Selma, Ala.: Times Book and Job Office.

HF 2003. 2003. *Adventures of Huckleberry Finn.* Edited by Victor Fischer and Lin Salamo, with the late Walter Blair. The Works of Mark Twain. Berkeley and Los Angeles: University of California Press. Also online at *MTPO.*

Holcombe, R. I., comp. 1884. *History of Marion County, Missouri, Written and Compiled from the Most Authentic Official and Private Sources.* St. Louis: E. F. Perkins. Citations are to the 1979 reprint edition, Hannibal: Marion County Historical Society.

Inds. 1989. *Huck Finn and Tom Sawyer among the Indians, and Other Unfinished Stories.* Foreword and notes by Dahlia Armon and Walter Blair. The Mark Twain Library. Berkeley and Los Angeles: University of California Press. Also online at *MTPO.*

Johnson, Robert U., and Clarence Clough Buel, eds. 1887–89. *Battles and Leaders of the Civil War.* 4 vols. New York: The Century Company.

Jones, Alexander E. 1954. "Mark Twain and Freemasonry." *American Literature* 26 (November): 363–73.

Kruse, Horst. 1981. *Mark Twain and "Life on the Mississippi."* Amherst: University of Massachusetts Press.

L1. 1988. *Mark Twain's Letters, Volume 1: 1853–1866.* Edited by Edgar Marquess Branch, Michael B. Frank, and Kenneth M. Sanderson. Berkeley: University of California Press. Also online at *MTPO.*

L6. 2002. *Mark Twain's Letters, Volume 6: 1874–1875*. Edited by Michael B. Frank and Harriet Elinor Smith. Berkeley: University of California Press. Also online at *MTPO*.

Lomax, John A., and Alan Lomax. 1934. *American Ballads and Folk Songs*. New York: Macmillan.

Lorch, Fred W. 1941. "Mark Twain and the 'Campaign That Failed.'" *American Literature* 12 (January): 454–70.

Loving, Jerome. 2013. *Confederate Bushwhacker: Mark Twain in the Shadow of the Civil War*. Hanover, N.H.: University Press of New England.

Mack, Effie Mona. 1947. *Mark Twain in Nevada*. New York: Charles Scribner's Sons.

Marleau, Michael H.
  2009. "'Cooling Our Bottom on the Sand Bars': A Chronicle of a Low Water Trip." Twainquotes.com. http://www. twainquotes.com/CoolingOurBottom.html. Accessed 5 February 2018.

  2015. "Sam Clemens, Steamboat Pilot for the Confederacy." *Mark Twain Journal* 53 (Spring): 69–87.

Mattson, J. Stanley.
  1968a. "Mark Twain on War and Peace: The Missouri Rebel and 'The Campaign that Failed.'" *American Quarterly* 20 (Winter): 783–94.

  1968b. "Twain's Last Months on the Mississippi." *Missouri Historical Review* 62 (July): 398–409.

McKinnon, William P. 2004. "'Unquestionably Authentic and Correct in Every Detail': Probing John I. Ginn and His Remarkable Utah War Story." *Utah Historical Quarterly* 72 (2004): 322–42.

McKivigan, John R. 2008. *Forgotten Firebrand: James Redpath and the Making of Nineteenth-Century America.* Ithaca, N.Y.: Cornell University Press.

MEC. Mary E. (Mollie) Clemens.

MEC. 1862. "Mrs. Orion Clemens. 'Journal.' For 1862." MS, location unknown. Photocopy in CU-MARK.

Messent, Peter. 2001. *The Short Works of Mark Twain: A Critical Study.* Philadelphia: University of Pennsylvania Press.

Missouri General Assembly. 2001. *An Act to Provide for the Organization, Government, and Support of the Military Forces, State of Missouri, Passed at the Called Session of the Twenty-First General Assembly.* Independence, Mo.: Two Trails Publishing, reprinting the original edition (Jefferson City: J. P. Ament, 1861).

MoHi. Missouri State Historical Society, Columbia, Mo.

MoSW. Washington University, St. Louis, Mo.

MS. Manuscript.

MTB. 1912. *Mark Twain: A Biography.* By Albert Bigelow Paine. 3 vols. New York: Harper and Brothers. Volume numbers in citations are to this edition; page numbers are the same in all editions.

MTBus. 1946. *Mark Twain, Business Man*. Edited by Samuel Charles Webster. Boston: Little, Brown and Company.

MTEnt. 1957. *Mark Twain of the* Enterprise. Edited by Henry Nash Smith, with the assistance of Frederick Anderson. Berkeley and Los Angeles: University of California Press.

MTLP. 1967. *Mark Twain's Letters to His Publishers, 1867–1894*. Edited by Hamlin Hill. The Mark Twain Papers. Berkeley and Los Angeles: University of California Press.

MTPO. *Mark Twain Project Online*. Edited by the Mark Twain Project. Berkeley and Los Angeles: University of California Press. http://www.marktwainproject.org.

N&J1. 1975. *Mark Twain's Notebooks and Journals, Volume 1 (1855–1873)*. Edited by Frederick Anderson, Michael B. Frank, and Kenneth M. Sanderson. The Mark Twain Papers. Berkeley and Los Angeles: University of California Press.

N&J2. 1975. *Mark Twain's Notebooks and Journals, Volume 2 (1877–1883)*. Edited by Frederick Anderson, Lin Salamo, and Bernard Stein. The Mark Twain Papers. Berkeley and Los Angeles: University of California Press.

N&J3. 1979. *Mark Twain's Notebooks and Journals, Volume 3 (1883–1891)*. Edited by Robert Pack Browning, Michael B. Frank, and Lin Salamo. The Mark Twain Papers. Berkeley and Los Angeles: University of California Press.

National Park Service. 1984. "National Register of Historic Places Inventory—Nomination Form" for Hannibal Central Business District. https://npgallery.nps.gov/GetAsset

/0a35804a-6643-4852-9fed-6175d2d3b4d2. Accessed 5 March 2018.

NPV. Vassar College, Poughkeepsie, N.Y.

OC. Orion Clemens.

OOxM. Walter Havighurst Special Collections, King Library, Miami University, Oxford, Ohio.

Orleans Census. 1860. *Population Schedules of the Eighth Census of the United States, 1860. Roll M653, 420. Louisiana: Orleans Parish, New Orleans, Ward 11.* Photocopy in CU-MARK.

OR. 1880–1901. *The War of the Rebellion: A Compilation of the Official Records of the Union and Confederate Armies.* 130 vols. Washington, D.C.: Government Printing Office.

Peckham, James. 1866. *Gen. Nathaniel Lyon, and Missouri in 1861. A Monograph of the Great Rebellion.* New York: American News Company.

Pettit, Arthur. 1974. *Mark Twain and the South.* Lexington: University Press of Kentucky.

Phillips, Christopher. 2000. *Missouri's Confederate: Claiborne Fox Jackson and the Creation of Southern Identity in the Border West.* Columbia: University of Missouri Press.

Plat Book of Ralls County. N.d. *Plat Book of Ralls County, Missouri.* Rockford, Ill.: W. W. Hixson and Co.

Portrait. 1895. *Portrait and Biographical Record of Marion, Ralls and Pike Counties, with a Few from Macon, Adair, and Lewis Counties, Missouri.* Chicago: C. O. Owen and Co. Citations are to the 1982 revised reprint edition, edited by Oliver Howard and Goldena Howard. New London, Mo.: Ralls County Book Company.

Price, Sterling. 1861. "Orders from Maj. Gen. Price." Orders dated 1 June. Liberty (Mo.) *Tribune*, 21 June, 1.

Rachels, David, ed. 2007. *Mark Twain's Civil War.* Lexington: University Press of Kentucky.

Ralls Census. 1850. *Population Schedules of the Seventh Census of the United States, 1850. Missouri: Ralls County.* National Archives Microfilms Publications, M432, Roll 424. Washington, D.C.: General Services Administration.

Ralls Census. 1860. *Population Schedules of the Eighth Census of the United States, 1860. Missouri: Ralls County.* National Archives Microfilms Publications, M653, Roll 642. Washington, D.C.: General Services Administration.

Raymond, M. D. 1887. *Gray Genealogy, Being a Genealogical Record and History of the Descendants of John Gray....*Tarrytown, N.Y.: M. D. Raymond.

Redpath, James. 1865. "The Tennessee Sergeants." *Harper's Weekly* 9 (7 October): 631.

RoBards, John Lewis. 1915. "Mark Twain as a Boy and a Man Who Made the World Laugh." Hannibal *Journal*, 27 June, clipping in RoBards Scrapbooks, vol. 3.

RoBards Scrapbooks. n.d. Scrapbooks compiled by John Lewis RoBards. 3 vols. Joint Collection, Western Historical

Manuscript Collection and the State Historical Society of Missouri Manuscripts, University of Missouri, Columbia.

Rule, G. E. 2002. "Tucker's War: Missouri and the Northwest Conspiracy." *Civil War St. Louis.* http://www.civilwarstlouis. com/History2/tuckerswar.htm#_ednref8. Accessed 20 August 2017.

S&B. 1967. *Mark Twain's Satires and Burlesques.* Edited with an introduction by Franklin R. Rogers. The Mark Twain Papers. Berkeley and Los Angeles: University of California Press.

Scharf, J. Thomas.
  1883. *History of Saint Louis City and County, from the Earliest Periods to the Present Day.* 2 vols. Philadelphia: Louis H. Everts and Co.
  1887. *History of the Confederate States Navy from Its Organization to the Surrender of Its Last Vessel.* New York: Rogers and Sherwood.

Scharnhorst, Gary. 2018. *The Life of Mark Twain: The Early Years, 1835–1871.* Columbia: University of Missouri Press.

Schmitz, Neil. 1995. "Mark Twain's Civil War: Humor's Reconstructive Writing." In *The Cambridge Companion to Mark Twain.* Edited by Forrest G. Robinson. Cambridge: Cambridge University Press.

Sherman, William T. 1875. *Memoirs of General William T. Sherman. By Himself.* 2 vols. New York: D. Appleton and Co.

Singer, Jane. 2005. *The Confederate Dirty War: Arson, Bombings, Assassination and Plots for Chemical and Germ Attacks on the Union.* Jefferson, N.C.: McFarland.

SLC (Samuel Langhorne Clemens).

1859. ["The Mysterious Murders in Risse."] MS in NPV. Published in *ET&S1*, 134–41.

1860. "Special River Correspondence." St. Louis *Missouri Republican*, 15 December, 4. Reprinted in Marleau 2009.

1875a. "Old Times on the Mississippi. II. A 'Cub' Pilot's Experience; or, Learning the River." *Atlantic Monthly* 35 (February): 217–24.

1875b. "Old Times on the Mississippi. III. The Continued Perplexities of 'Cub' Piloting." *Atlantic Monthly* 35 (March): 283–89.

1875c. "Old Times on the Mississippi. IV. The 'Cub' Pilot's Education Nearly Completed." *Atlantic Monthly* 35 (April): 446–52.

1875d. "Old Times on the Mississippi. V. 'Sounding.' Faculties Peculiarly Necessary to a Pilot." *Atlantic Monthly* 35 (May): 567–74.

1875e. "Old Times on the Mississippi. VI. Official Rank and Dignity of a Pilot. The Rise and Decadence of the Pilots' Association." *Atlantic Monthly* 35 (June): 721–30.

1877. "Our Military Guests. The Ancients and Honorables." Hartford *Courant*, 3 October, 2. Reprinted in this volume as Appendix A.

1883. *Life on the Mississippi.* Boston: James R. Osgood and Co.

1887. "Twain as a Soldier. His Speech to Union Veterans."
Baltimore *American*, 9 April, 4. Reprinted in Fatout
1976, 219–21.

1892. *Merry Tales*. New York: Charles L. Webster and Co.

1896. *The American Claimant, and Other Stories and
Sketches*. New York: Harper and Brothers.

1897. *Following the Equator: A Journey around the World*.
Hartford, Conn.: American Publishing Company.

1899. "Concerning the Jews." *Harper's New Monthly Magazine*
99 (September): 527–35. Reprinted in *The Man That
Corrupted Hadleyburg and Other Stories and Essays* (New
York: Harper and Brothers, 1900).

1901. "Lincoln and the Civil War. (Address by Mr. Clemens
at the Lincoln birthday celebration in Carnegie Hall,
New York, February 11th, 1901)." In Brewer 1902,
3846–48.

1910. *Mark Twain's Speeches*. New York: Harper and Brothers.

1923. *Mark Twain's Speeches*. With an introduction by
Albert Bigelow Paine. New York: Harper and Brothers.

Snead, Thomas L. 1886. *The Fight for Missouri: From the Election
of Lincoln to the Death of Lyon*. New York: Charles Scribner's
Sons.

Stevens, Walter B. 1915. *Missouri: The Center State, 1821–1915*.
4 vols. Chicago: S. J. Clarke Publishing Company.

Stone, Mary Beth.
1980a. "Information about Daniel Ralls." *Mary Beth Stone
Family*. http://www.genealogy.com/ftm/s/t/o/Mary-B-

Stone/WEBSITE-0001/UHP-1695.html. Accessed 17 August 2017.

1980b. "Information about John Ralls." *Mary Beth Stone Family*. http://www.genealogy.com/ftm/s/t/o/Mary-B-Stone/WEBSITE-0001/UHP-1864.html. Accessed 17 August 2017.

Tenney, Thomas A., ed. 1998. "Interviews with Horace Bixby." *Mark Twain Journal* 36 (Spring): 34–40.

TS. Typescript.

U.S. House of Representatives.

1866. *Report of the Joint Committee on Reconstruction, at the First Session Thirty-Ninth Congress. Part IV: Florida, Louisiana, Texas*. Washington, D.C.: Government Printing Office.

1876. *Index to the Miscellaneous Documents of the House of Representatives for the First Session of the Forty-Fourth Congress*. Washington, D.C.: Government Printing Office.

U.S. Senate.

1876. Report of the Committee on Naval Affairs, no. 420. *Report of Committees of the Senate of the United States for the First Session of the Forty-Fourth Congress, 1875–'76, Volume 3*. Washington, D.C.: Government Printing Office.

1877. Report of the Committee on Naval Affairs, no. 638. *Report of Committees of the Senate of the United States*

for the Second Session of the Forty-Fourth Congress, 1876–
'77, Volume 1. Washington, D.C.: Government Printing Office.

1902. *Missouri Troops in Service during the Civil War. Letter to*
the Secretary of War. 57th Congress, 1st Session, Document No. 412. Washington, D.C.: Government Printing Office.

ViU. University of Virginia, Charlottesville.

Webster, Annie Moffett. 1918. "Family Chronicle Written for
Jean Webster McKinney by her Grandmother." Typescript,
dated 26 October, in NPV. Photocopy in CU-MARK.

Williams, Walter, ed. 1913. *A History of Northeast Missouri.* 3
vols. Chicago: Lewis Publishing Company.

WIM. 1973. *What Is Man? and Other Philosophical Writings.*
Edited by Paul Baender. The Works of Mark Twain. Berkeley and Los Angeles: University of California Press.

Benjamin Griffin is an editor at the Mark Twain Project, which is housed within the Mark Twain Papers at the University of California, Berkeley. A Berkeley native, he was educated there and at Cambridge University. In addition to Mark Twain, he specializes in the theory and practice of scholarly editing.